Earth Runnings, Revelations and Grace

Life Experiences Biblically Explored

Mindy M. Tucker

Trilogy Christian Publishers
A Wholly Owned Subsidiary of Trinity Broadcasting Network
2442 Michelle Drive
Tustin, CA 92780

Cover design by: Cornerstone Creative Solutions

For information, address Trilogy Christian Publishing
Rights Department, 2442 Michelle Drive, Tustin, Ca 92780.
Trilogy Christian Publishing/ TBN and colophon are trademarks of Trinity Broadcasting Network.

For information about special discounts for bulk purchases, please contact Trilogy Christian Publishing.

Manufactured in the United States of America

10 9 8 7 6 5 4 3 2 1

Library of Congress Cataloging-in-Publication Data is available.

ISBN 978-1-64773-957-7 (Print Book)
ISBN 978-1-64773-958-4 (ebook)

Dedication

To all who supported and believed in my ability.

Contents

Acknowledgements

God is an awesome God! I thank Him for my abilities.

"Your destiny is tied to your talent."

These words from a former Youth Pastor have inspired and challenged me over the years. They have allowed me to fail, pick myself up, and try again. The road travelled has been inspiring, thought-provoking, and rocky at times. However, without the support and love of family and friends, I would not have been able to complete this book. My heartfelt appreciation to S. Tucker and R. Dixon for their unending patience and time given to the book's development.

Sincere gratitude is to be extended to my readers that kept the message on point through many revisions: Mike Giovanni Resnik, Rev. Audrey Manning, and E. Hampton. To those who kept me covered with prayer at every point during this process: K. Sinclair, Hazel Reid and N. Watson.

To all the youth leaders, teachers, and pastors that have crossed my path and poured into my life throughout the years, my immense gratitude. Lastly, but not least, to my die-hard supporters who constantly checked in on my progress. You guys know who you are, thank you and God Bless.

Foreword

Earth Runnings, Revelations and Grace is a riveting book that highlights the sinful nature plaguing our world and society as the author articulates this through personal stories. In essence, it is a stark reminder of the revolutionary cultural battle the world faces as we increasingly move away from biblical truths. The Bible is the only book that answers the four questions of living, namely, the origins of life (beginning), the meaning of life (purpose), moral absolutes (worldview), and the destiny of individuals after death (eternity or non-existence). However, to solve the cultural and social issues we face, as spoken about within these pages, we can look no further than the pages of the Bible. Therefore, to understand the problem, we must first understand its beginning, as humanity continues to trample and erode any need for God.

Many are lost in a sea of hopelessness and despair, as the author pointedly depicts. The nuclear family, in large part, is non-existing or has already surrendered to the whims and fancies of secular humanism, administrative control, and modulating the pursuit of a relationship with God. The family structure that was once solid has now become an unknowing participant in the demise of foundational truths, grasping paths, and realities that claim to satisfy. However, these ungodly presuppositions only lead to more bondage and fear, as the book portrays. *Earth Runnings, Revelations and Grace* paints a cultural picture about life that can only be summed up in four words: "humanity's need for God."

The only way to solve the issues highlighted within these pages is to return to biblically foundational-based principles. What then? Do we lose hope as we see our families ravaged by a changing world? No! We fight back with grace. We inform the masses to turn their gaze upward to God to solve life's concerns. The response lies in the need to recognize the fact that the scriptures contains the answers to life's queries and challenges. *Earth Runnings, Revelations and Grace* will not disappoint the reader because it speaks truths about life and the societal issues affecting our world. Now is the time to speak the truth in love.

Mike Giovanni Resnik

Preface

This book in essence is a dream, years delayed.

I always spoke of writing a book about my life experiences. So, I collected memories, hoping to put pen to paper one day. However, life happened, and the book receded into the recesses of my mind. As I travelled, I realized the disparities between societies, and the passion to put pen to paper began flickering. However, time became my enemy as there never seemed to be enough hours in a day. I would jot ideas down over the years, but the book never materialized. I contemplated what to write and how to go about writing it with each draft collecting dust. Once again, I became flustered, and the dream was delayed.

God works in mysterious ways; I was laid off from my job, and months later, the Coronavirus pandemic materialized. I realized this was a call to action and was inspired to put awareness for *Earth Runnings, Revelations and Grace* on paper. The God of Abraham and Isaac is still the God of today; although seldom explored, He never changes. It is in this period where I began reflecting on my life experiences and realized that, as God was with Jonah and Elisha, so too is He with me.

I trust that, as you read the pages, you experience moments of levity, inspiration, blessings, and a challenge to look inward. The hope is that a glimmer of purpose gets ignited in your life as our days on Earth are numbered.

Introduction

Are you hot, cold, or lukewarm for God?

What is our purpose on Earth?

Do we live to die?

These are questions which we have all asked over the years as the composition of reality changes from generation to generation, the basic principle remains the same.

Why am I on Earth?

As with each new generation, our moral compass has gradually shifted away from the Word of God. The light which should emanate from believers in Jesus Christ has been constantly flickering, with our foundation gradually eroding. Our moral compasses have embraced the tenets of compromise and self-exultation, which have swiftly gained footholds in our lives. Many of these footholds have unknowingly created entryways for diabolic forces.

Earth Runnings, Revelations and Grace is a personal and cultural snapshot of social topics versus biblical truths. It addresses the issue of racism and culture shock upon my arrival in the United States of America. Also, subjects such as the breakdown of marriage, what constitutes a marriage, and the questioning of one's sexuality. The material covered also allows for self-examination of purpose and how to improve as individuals.

Each topic addressed is used to challenge, inspire, and encourage individuals to direct their moral compasses closer to God's truth. The modalities used to share my life experiences are told in stories and poems to establish a basic innate truth that we are frail humans. The foundational pillars of faith, obedience, compassion, prayer, and gratitude are examined with candor and humor. The injection of bible stories helps to emphasize the fact that God never changes from Genesis to present day.

Why the title *Earth Runnings, Revelations and Grace*, you might ask?

I surmise many of us enter our days in a state of angst and barely enough thought is given to God, our Creator. Earth Runnings is simply a term I use for daily happenings. This topic was chosen as a reminder to us that God is in control of our daily lives. Our time on Earth is measured and should be used wisely with the knowledge that only what we do for Christ will stand the test of time. Each day, He reveals Himself and exposes areas in our lives which need His attention and offers Grace and Mercy.

God is unchanging in a changing world.

Talk with Jesus

"Then you will call on me and come and
pray to me, and I will listen to you."
Jeremiah 29:12 NIV

A talk with Jesus.

Can you speak with Jesus directly?

In some instances, there are individuals that will answer "No" to that question. However, I know you can communicate in this manner. The elders would tell us as children that we needed to keep God close in prayer. They encouraged this form of interaction as it offered an open connection to our Heavenly Father. There are many ways we may communicate with God outside of prayer. Song, dance, poetry, music, and drama are a few other avenues which are often used. However, the most intimate of these access channels is prayer. This conduit was introduced to me in depth as an adolescent at my church camp.

The Power of Prayer

Years ago, at the beginning of cordless technology, I would always find myself in embarrassing situations. As people constantly walked by me talking and seeing no one around, I would always answer the person passing by. Many individuals would often look at me with annoyed looks. Some would point to their ears, and sometimes others would wave their fingers as an indication that I was not the intended recipient of their words. Hard to imagine those days, as this form of communication is now the normal way of life. People no longer think you are "crazy" for speaking to yourself, as technology has far advanced to wireless connection.

I thought about my personal encounters and realized that I often had conversations with God. In those instances, I can only imagine how I was viewed by individuals, as there was no technology sticking out of my ears. I was having normal conversations, laughing, smiling, and crying. It would appear to someone passing by at the time that I was conversing with myself. I was, in fact, having a little talk with God.

The final church camp I attended in my homeland introduced me to a theme created by the leaders asserting the importance of a talk with Jesus: "*Prayer... Power unlimited*!" In those seven enlightening days, the foundation for prayer was laid. Prayer is having a chat or communing with God. I was of the belief as a young child that, in order to have a talk with God, you had to use many words. It had to be long, you had to use big words, be respectful, and sometimes you would have to speak loudly for God to hear. These myths were soon dispelled as I learned that it was easy to communicate with God. He did not require you to have a production.

My mom's response to what I termed a "Production Prayer" is explained in this manner, "It's not about being holier than thou or going up like Elijah and dropping like old pan." I suspect Mom got this saying from our local vernacular or my grandmother. Meaning, God responds in the simplest of manner. He does not need a Broadway performance to get His attention. Elijah, in his time of need and despair, had a simple interaction with God.

Elijah and the Still Small Voice

The prophet Elijah learned that God often communicates in a still small voice. After he destroyed Baal, the god of Jezebel threatened to kill him, and he became afraid. Elijah ran to the cave and prayed for death. While in that cave, he received a word from God asking what his reason was for being in the cave. Once God heard his reason for hiding, the heavenly response was the following:

> And he said, Go forth, and stand upon the mount before the Lord, And, behold the Lord passed by, and a great and strong wind rent the mountains, and brake in pieces the rocks before the Lord; but the Lord was not in the wind: and after the wind an earthquake; but the Lord was not in the earthquake: And after the earthquake a fire; but the Lord was not in the fire; and after the fire a still small voice. And it was so, when Elijah heard it that he wrapped his face in his mantle, and went out, and stood in the entering of the cave. And, behold, there came a voice unto him and said, What doest thou here, Elijah?
>
> 1 Kings 19:11-13

God did not make a great entrance in any of the weather-related systems; He communicated in a still small voice with Elijah—not in a major theater production manner. Have there been instances where you have missed the presence of God because you were expecting a showcase?

Personal Communication with God

I believed that God only listened when you made a production of prayer. I would sometimes wonder about the manner in which my colleagues prayed. Often, I would hear them give varying testimonial reports of the supernatural power of God during services. One person would testify to a devastating medical diagnosis. However, weeks later they would say the doctors looked at the report, and the individual was given a clean bill of health. Other times, I would hear of someone being robbed, saying a prayer in the moment, and the thief running away. I thought, *How is it that I did not get these responses to my prayers in the form of a big supernatural production?* Consequently, I did get these responses, but I was blinded to them; I had forgotten God's years of divine interventions in my life.

Many individuals, when they pray, ask for healing, spiritual deliverance, improved finances, a house, a job, or a partner for marriage. I decided to pray for challenges and trials. The belief was, if I got the challenges, my testimonials relayed would be supernatural like my colleagues. The reality that I was alive each morning, had my faculties intact, had food, shelter, and could smell the rain did not factor into my equation of supernatural. Please be careful what you pray for. After that, prayer things became overwhelming, and soon my prayer became "Okay, God, I get it. Can you stop the madness?" The point is, God listens to our prayers and answers in ways which we often ignore. Never underestimate your communication with God.

Production Prayer

One of Jesus' disciples asked Him to teach them to pray, and Jesus responded by instructing them in what we know as the Lord's Prayer found in Luke 11:1-4. In essence, Jesus Christ was saying be earnest and honest in your talk with God, ask for His forgiveness, and be willing to forgive those that have wronged you. Our approach and attitude towards prayer should be reflected in our treatment of our fellow man.

I once heard of a story involving two church members. One member recently migrated from the Caribbean region. The other member was fully established within the United States and respected within the church. The well-known church member was renowned for her "Production Prayers." She would constantly make a showcase whenever she was asked to pray. The other member was modest, took the bus, and was dealing with a new culture. The issue at hand was that they lived in close proximity of each other, but the established church member, who had a vehicle, never offered the new member a ride to church.

> *Was the established church member her sister's keeper?*

A prayerful person should always be mindful of the needs of others.

*****

Food for Thought: Prayer is power unrestricted, as it gives us open access to God. He is not caught up in the details and showcase; instead, He needs a humble heart in His presence.

God might not come in the form we expect, but He will always listen and respond. If our motives are not pure, no amount of beseeching will get God's attention. "If a man say, I love God, and hateth his brother, he is a liar: for he that loveth not his brother whom he hath seen, how can he love God whom he hath not seen?" (1 John 4:20).

The Good Samaritan

Jamaican Proverb: "Scarnful dawg nyam dutty pudding."
Translation: Scornful dog eat dirty pudding.
Explanation: People who are haughty are soon humbled or be mindful not to judge others.

"You were a champion of compassion
You had no problem helping Lillian
Society saw a 'mad' woman you saw a friend
When I would hide on Sundays as you approached
You would say "Scarnful dawg nyam dutty pudding"

These words are from a poem I wrote for my mother on Mother's Day in 2018. She truly embodies the spirit of the Good Samaritan, a bastion of compassion. When I was growing up, the individuals who lived on the streets in tattered clothing or no clothing, had terrible personal hygiene practices, were labeled as a "mad" person. I often questioned how they ended up living on the streets, but the answers I received were never quite good enough. As a child, I did a lot of performing, and, as a result of these performances, many children's homes and centers were assisted. However, it was my mom who planted the seed of compassion.

Mom and Lillian

On a personal level, homelessness and mental illness were always within my surroundings. My high school was across the street from what was, at the time, the largest mental health hospital in the English-speaking Caribbean. During the holiday season, my music teacher would escort us across the street to the hospital to perform for the patients. I encountered these individuals, who would be termed homeless in the United states, daily as I commuted. Caring for the mentally ill, at that time in my homeland, carried a stigma in the society. Mom always questioned the behavior of others who treated the "mad" people less than human. She took care of everyone whom she met that needed assistance—her kindness knew no bounds. I often wondered if she understood that she could not save the world.

Mom and I would go to church on Sunday mornings, and it was on these visits that my mother would perform one of her many acts of kindness. There was a lady, her name was Lillian. She was classified as a "mad" person because she was dirty and unkempt and lived on the streets. My mother took care of this lady every Sunday by bringing her money, food, clothing, or material for clothing along with needle and thread. Lillian and mom would have fascinating conversations about life and Lillian's safety. It was realized that Lillian was once a teacher; she was highly intelligent and funny. I am not sure what the circumstances were which led to her being on the streets, but I know she was a remarkable woman.

Whenever my mother was unable to make the trip to church on Sundays, I or one of my siblings would deliver the supplies to Lillian. There were some Sundays when Mom and I would see Lillian, and her face would be bruised and swollen. She would tell us she had been abused by the boys on the street. I felt empathy towards her, but I was also aware of my surrounding and made the conversation quick. A sense of shame would take hold of me. I did not want to be seen giving supplies to Lillian, as I did not want to be labeled by society as someone who kept company with a "mad woman."

Mortified to be seen with Lillian

During the school week, I would see Lillian sitting on the street side. Most days, I was in uniform and in the company of my friends, and I would hide. My friends would not have said anything derogatory towards Lillian, but I did not want to be associated with her. At that time in history, my high school was mostly known for its athletic prowess, and the fact that the "mad house" was in front of our school. So, being seen with her would further perpetuate the sentiment that, as students, we too were "mad" or often communicated with the mentally ill.

Whenever I told my mom about these encounters, she never chided but gave wise counsel. My mother soon set me straight with her arguments of compassion, humility, and love. "We are all here to help each other," my mom would say. "None of us is better than the other." She would repeat the famous Jamaican proverb, "*Scarnful dawg nyam dutty pudding*." I accepted that Lillian was not "mad," as she often told me to be good and stay in school.

I see Lillian now in my mind's eye. Sitting on the street corner with a slight hunch to her posture. Her bundles piled high behind her on the dirty sidewalk. Her clothing is semi-clean, depending on her outfit that day. She took pleasure and pride in using the materials Mom delivered. There is thread hanging from each ear lobes to keep her piercings open. The shoes on her feet are torn and well-worn. Her face is weathered and tired from years on the street or slightly bruised, depending on her week. Lillian's hairstyle is plaited in a design all her own. Her hands are lined with wrinkles as she stretches them towards Mom and says, "God Bless You."

She was always smiling as Mom approached her. Lillian was thankful for the minutes she spent with Mom. In that time and space, she was not a label which society had given her but a friend. Her smile stands out in my memory, and so do the words of my mother, "You are only one paycheck away from being homeless." Years later, I would reflect on the contact with Lillian, and counted it as a blessing.

Good Samaritan

Lillian's story always reminded me of the Good Samaritan in Luke 10:30-37. Jesus spoke of a man traveling from Jerusalem to Jericho; he was confronted by bandits. The man was undressed, robbed, trounced, and left for dead. The parable goes on to tell of two religious men who came along the side of the road. They each saw him agonizing and ignored him. A third man came by; he stopped to help the injured man. He was someone who society labelled as an outcast, a Samaritan. This third individual displayed sympathy towards him. He cleansed and bound his wounds, placed him on his animal, and transported him to an Inn in the care of the inn keeper. Once the Samaritan checked out of the inn the next day, he paid the bill for the injured man and instructed the innkeeper that further cost would be paid whenever he returned to this area of the country. I often look at the irony of this parable. Someone that was labelled an outcast by society was the only one who sought to help a fellow human in need. Yet, individuals who society held in high esteem refused to help.

> *How many of you ignore the needs of an individual because you are afraid of society's response?*

Practice What You Preach

As a teenager, I was active in church activities, especially camps and youth fellowships. One Sunday evening stood out as we had a visiting youth leader, Phillip. It was our scheduled Music Appreciation Night at our youth fellowship. We were asked to bring in different songs from various artistes to be analyzed. These were the days of cassettes, vinyl records, and the cassette deck. One of my colleagues brought in "Another Day in Paradise" on cassette, written and sung by Phil Collins. This was a very popular song on the airwaves at the time. After we finished analyzing the song, I gained a new perspective on the piece. Our youth leader issued a challenge to us, "Don't just listen to the words of the song, practice what it says." We sat, ate, listened to several other songs, and had a good fellowship. Many of us left with the thought process that we should be alert to the content of songs and not just the beat of the song.

The songs discussed left our memory as we prepared to head home. Phillip walked with members of the youth group towards our bus stop. On the way to the bus stop, we saw a man begging on the roadside. We kept walking as a group. Phillip stopped and said, "So what are you guys going to do?" We were initially confused. Then, I understood what he meant in his prior discussion. Compassion is key, we should strive to practice what we preach. We donated money to the beggar and became pensive. Some will say we were manipulated into giving, but I would rebut that. It gave us a feeling of gratitude that we could improve the circumstance of someone that was in need.

*****

Food for Thought: Compassion and understanding are values well to be exercised daily. Jesus made it clear while speaking with His disciples that we should care for one another, as this is the second greatest commandment: "And the second is like unto it, Thou shalt love thy neighbors as thyself" (Matthew 22:39).

Sands of Time

By Mindy Tucker

In order to move forward we must look back
As we sift the sands of time
We stand and think about time and space
Dimensions which are gingerly held by
the delicate notion of the future
You have said the word fate and left me to contemplate
The varying degree of our existence
We sit and ponder but then why wonder
As our state of affairs have already been written
In the sands of time
We exude a level of concern and yet deep
within the nuances of our very soul
We learned never to question
Our emotions lay within the recesses of our minds
As we watch the blowing sands of time
The essence of our being spew forth the
unexplained and the unexplored
A thousand words have already echoed from our lips
In the moments of silence
As we stand and gaze at the sands of time
We play with music and words
We say the unsaid and trust it will be heard
Much to be voiced but not enough time left to say it
We weigh all our directions and options
As we remember our sands of time

Foundation of Faith

"I am thy servant; give me understanding,
that I may know thy testimonies."
Psalm 119:125

Without faith, it is hopeless to please God!

"Now faith is the substance of things hoped for, the evidence of things not seen" (Hebrews 11:1). Faith is often misunderstood, as there is not an earthly way to measure it. The parable is told by Jesus of the Kingdom of God being equated to a mustard seed. Have you ever seen a mustard seed? It is one of the smallest seeds in the herb family. However, when that seed is planted, it becomes a great tree. Likewise, if we cultivated and activated faith in our personal lives, we would be giants for Christ. "And the Lord said, If ye had faith as a grain of mustard seed, ye might say unto this sycamine tree, Be thou plucked up by the root, and thou planted in the sea; and it should obey you" (Luke 17:6). Many of us struggle with the fact that we have this power within us.

Hebrews 11 is considered the Hall of Fame of Faith; it contains the names of the "Who is Who" of the Bible. These individuals all had faults, but they were known for trusting in God's Word. In examining faith, I would like to look at Abraham and the mandate to sacrifice his son Isaac, and Elisha and the widow woman with the cruse of oil. Also, how we interpret faith in our daily lives.

Abraham's Faith in God

God told Abram that his name would be changed and would be the father of many nations. The proclamation from God went further as He told Abraham that his wife at ninety would have a child. Abraham did not believe this to be true, so he laughed and fell on his face. In his finite mind, it was not possible as he was one hundred years old. He reacted in disbelief to the impending birth of his child, thereby doubting God. However, God told Abraham the name of his child would be Isaac (Genesis 17). Today, I would envision Abraham as a multimillionaire with many ranch houses, lots of cattle, acres of land, fruitful trees, and many employees. God never lies, and the prophecy of Isaac's birth was fulfilled. However, God had a test of faith for Abraham to pass. God commanded him to offer Isaac, his precious son, as a sacrifice.

> And he said, Take now thy son, thine only son Isaac, whom thou lovest, and get thee into the land of Moriah; and offer him there for a burnt offering upon one of the mountains which I will tell thee of. And Abraham rose up early in the morning; and saddled his ass, and took two of his young men with him and Isaac his son, and clave the wood for the burnt offering, and rose up and went unto the place of which God had told him
>
> Genesis 22:2-3

There are two aspects which are highlighted in the retelling of Abraham's story:

1. Isaac willingly followed his dad and trusted that there would be a sacrificial lamb provided based on his father's word.
2. Abraham obeyed God and was willing to sacrifice his beloved son knowing that God would provide a sacrificial lamb based on His prior promises.

What!
How is that possible?
What an enormous display of faith.

As Abraham prepared to sacrifice Isaac, he asked his father, "Where is your offering?" Abraham answered without a doubt that God would provide. As he prepared to sacrifice his son Isaac, God told Abraham not to hurt him. Instead, God provided a ram caught in the thicket for Abraham's use. He never once questioned God as he knew God had previously provided for him, and He never failed to deliver. He called the name of that place *Jehovah Jireh*, meaning my provider. Father and son personified the phrase "Faith in Action."

Elisha and the Widow with the Cruse of Oil

The economic downturns, stock losses, and collapsing housing markets have affected many households and placed many in debt and emotional turmoil in modern day society. Many individuals have turned to the government for assistance in clearing their debt. However, having a financial crisis is not a new experience. There was a widow who was experiencing financial trouble in the days of Elisha. In order to clear her balance, the bill collectors wanted her sons as bond servants for payment. She was clearly distraught about her debt and the possibility that her sons would be given into servitude. As a caring mother would do, she sought an outlet for assistance. The mother asked the prophet Elisha for help with her predicament.

> And Elisha said unto her, What shall I do for thee? tell me, what hast thou in the house? And she said, Thine handmaid hath not any thing in the house, save a pot of oil. Then he said, Go, borrow thee vessels abroad of all thy neighbours, even empty vessels; borrow not a few. And when thou art come in, thou shalt shut the door upon thee and upon thy sons, and shalt pour out into all those vessels, and thou shalt set aside that which is full.
> 2 Kings 4:2-4

The widow and her sons did as they were told to do by the prophet Elisha. They collected and borrowed every possible empty vessel and filled it to capacity with oil. Many might ask today, how are empty vessels going to erase her debt? However, their display of faith turned a pot of oil into many vessels of oil. The widow and her sons were able to sell the containers with oil to satisfy her debts. Having achieved a clear balance on her billing record, she was able to live with her sons in peace. The widow displayed immense faith and knew the prophet Elisha had a fear of the Lord. She knew God would provide for her needs more than she imagined.

Would you have followed Elisha's instruction without question?

The Audacity to Doubt God

I recall standing in the lobby of my prior church in New Jersey and having the most fascinating conversation with a former church member. We were of one mind. Creative minds that thought outside the box when it came to the stage and fashion. Our conversation revolved around faith and why it was so hard to enact it. He stared at me with a calm expression and a slight smile. He proclaimed one of the most profound statements in my recent memory:

Who or what gives us the audacity to doubt God?

I stared at him with a quizzical expression and tried to process the clarity with which he had simply addressed the subject of faith. We have heard of countless acts of faith throughout the Bible, most of which would make us crumble today. I think our misconception of faith is amplified because, for the most part, we think it does not apply to us as it applied to Abraham, Noah, and Moses. The God they worshipped then is the same God today. We display a form of daily belief, we may call it counterfeit faith, but we do display a form of trust:

- We get in our cars daily and trust that they will start.
- We ride trains over massive bodies of waters and bridges and trust that they will withstand the weight of tons of steel.

- We place our belief in the latest diet craze because it was recommended by a celebrity.
- We order food from restaurants to give ourselves nourishment not knowing how it was prepared.

Faith in Action

The engine of the car, tons of steel for the bridges and train, the credibility of a celebrity, the rating of a restaurant are all concrete elements which can be seen and measured. Yet, we never doubt that the train or car will transport us because it fulfils that job daily. So, we become comfortable with our daily activities. In doing so, we display a level of confidence which dismisses God from the equation of our lives. However, the faith that God requires from us is that belief, "Even though I cannot see you, I will trust you."

In times like these, we should look to the birds of the air that procure food without the level of our intelligence. The flowers that grow wild in their variegated coloring and scents without thought for their tomorrow. It is that blind trust that is needed to please God. The trust that says I do not have much food in the house, nor money for rent or transportation. However, you praise God in your circumstance, and it is in this praising that brings a knock on the door. In that knock, the brother of Faith, which is Hope, is manifested. It is a friend saying that they have been thinking about you with groceries for your empty pantry. Faith is not in the manifestation of the food but in the heart-felt praise and belief that God would provide even when you did not see a way out.

As a child, I loved singing about Father Abraham with his many sons and Jehovah Jireh our provider. I loved the action and movement in the songs, but as a youngster, the concept of faith had not yet taken root. There are times when I failed to believe, and I opened the door to fear by doubting God and bending to stress. In doing so, I had forgotten the prior deliverance and the awesomeness of God. The belief that God is present though unseen, and it is in the absence of concrete evidence that our faith manifests itself.

> *How many times have you fallen into this pothole of disbelief?*
>
> *If you ponder the God who created the human body and the galaxies, how can you doubt Him?*

We often forget that the world operates from a temporal perspective, but God is eternal. He is not like man; He never changes. So, once again in the words of my wise friend,

> *Who or what gives us the audacity to doubt God?*

*****

*Food for Thought***:** Faith is being able to recollect the goodness of God. It is the ability to proceed in the face of despair without crumbling, knowing that provisions are already being made for your life. Faith is the key to open the doors to belief and hope. There is always a ram waiting in the bushes.

Palm of God's Hands

"Behold, I have graven thee upon the palms of my hands; thy walls are continually before me."

Isaiah 49:16

I love the creative arts as I believe it builds character and responsibility. I loved being on stage, but other aspects of my life often suffered because of this interest. Whether it was schoolwork, friendships, or church activities, my acting came first. I performed publicly for the first time at my Preparatory School Prize Giving Ceremony, which would be equivalent to today's graduation ceremony. I knew then that the stage would be a place to escape and relax. However, I was getting ready to begin a new chapter in my academic life. I was not excited about high school. The fact is, I was terrified to be on this new path as I did not want to go where it was leading me.

School Days

I had the privilege of enjoying a world class education in what is classified as a "Third World" country. The curriculum would appear overwhelming to outsiders, but to me, it laid a foundation that was unparalleled. The thought of entering high school was overwhelming. I attended a preparatory school which had a total population of approximately ninety students. We were a close-knit family. Now, I would attend a school with a population of hundreds of pupils.

In the first semester of my high school, the material for our uniforms was on back order, so we had to wear white, brown, or black skirts with a white top. When we were able to wear the correct uniform, it was called "tablecloth" by the public. I constantly had to explain which school I attended because the plaid material was new. It was a type of gingham cotton plaid. I was mortified and wished I could be wearing any other uniform but the one which I was assigned. In those times, I would say, "Why did I have to attend this school?" Although, I did my research and learned that my new school produced world class scholars, scientists, entertainers, lawyers, and athletes, I had an issue with the location.

I made a connection with another student who appeared just as uncomfortable as I was during the first week of school. Her aunt was unsatisfied with her niece being placed in this school. Consequently, she arranged for her niece to be transferred to another high school in Kingston. So, within a week of starting school, my new friend was gone. I was left to handle all my new emotions. I felt like a fish out of water and often expressed my uneasiness to my mother.

My high school was in area of town which had pockets of violence and was located across the street from a mental hospital. My previous school environment was in what could be compared to a well-funded school district. The exposure to this new environment made me uncomfortable. My mother, in her infinite wisdom, shared words of calm and encouragement, "The education you receive at this high school will just be just as good as anywhere else. Whether you go to school uptown or downtown, your responsibility is to get a good education. Ignore what others say." To compound my situation, my science teacher, school nurse, school chaplain, and principal all attended the same church with me.

Within a year, I became comfortable with my surroundings; Mom was proven correct once again. I made new friends and got involved in various organizations. The first three years of high school I carried a heavy course load. So, I was ecstatic when I discovered I would be able to do drama classes. Music and drama classes were interchangeable for each term. Drama classes were my avenue to escape the heavy academic load. My high school was blessed with two of Jamaica's gifted theatrical talents as drama teachers. They displayed different styles, but I was able to soak up the knowledge each shared. I was handed an audition flyer by one of my drama teachers. He thought I should audition for a Performing Arts Club which was looking for new members. At the time, this club was the first of its kind on the island.

On the appointed day of the audition, my friend Rachel went with me. We arrived for the early morning engagement and were faced with a sea of faces. Hundreds of talented young people were present from all walks of life. I was stunned. Apparently, I had no idea what I had signed up for. All I kept saying to myself was, "What did I get myself into?" and "These guys are going eat me alive." As Rachel and I waited, the current members of the club oversaw controlling the flow of new applicants. We kept hearing them jokingly say, "Don't call us we will call you," which contributed to my bundle of nerves. Upon auditioning, I came face to face with juggernauts of Jamaican theater, music, and dance. I was accepted as a member of the performing arts club.

My Protectors: Robert and the Lady by the Fence

My performing arts troupe was rehearsing on the compound of the Jamaica School of Drama as we prepared for our upcoming concert season. Dancing was not my best attribute, so when my portion of rehearsal was completed, I decided to head home. The route which I would have taken to the bus stop was lined with trees, bushes, and poor street lighting. At that time of night, it was not advised for a young lady to be walking alone or anyone for that matter.

As I exited the compound, three young men were approaching from the direction of the National Stadium, which showcased many of our nation's athletes. They stopped and asked me the time. I replied, and they went on their way. The boys totally forgotten from my mind, I crossed the street, focused on getting home. Across the street from my rehearsal venue was the Little Theater, a beacon on the Jamaican theater scene. As I got to the sidewalk on the other side, I heard a voice coming from inside the cross-link fence of the Little Theater. I kept walking, but the person kept calling.

At the time, I was wearing my uniform t-shirt for my performing arts club and figured the lady wanted to know about tickets for our upcoming season. As I walked over, she had a concerned look on her face. I was accustomed to being stopped and asked about tickets or show times, so before she said anything, I said "The season doesn't begin yet. I have no idea about the ticket prices." She gently shook her head and informed me that she had no interest in tickets. She then said, "I have been watching you from across the street, and I saw when those boys approached you." The lady proceeded to ask that I look at the opposite side of the street. To my surprise, the three young men who I had told the time were standing near one of the trees along the poorly lit path which led to my bus stop. She further voiced, "After they spoke with you, they stopped by the tree. I think they were waiting for you to pass them; God knows what they had in mind." My knees felt weak upon hearing her observations. She called her friend to help me, his name was Robert.

Robert worked backstage on theatrical productions and coincidently was the uncle of a close friend. He was surprised to see me and pressed for time, as he was getting ready for the beginning of his night's duty. His friend explained what happened prior to him being called over to us. He was both angry and concerned. Although having no time to spare, he ran with me to my bus stop like we were being chased by a pride of lions. Years later, I thought about this event in my life. I figured, *What are the odds, that Robert and the woman would be in that place at that time?* God has a way of knowing what we need before we do. He is not a God of chance. He is a sovereign God and is always in control. He knows our life's path before we are born. As we are engraved in the palm of His hands.

Elijah, Jezebel, and the Angel

Elijah and Jezebel had a discordant affiliation. Jezebel was an evil individual who was married to King Ahab. She was responsible for leading the children of Israel into idolatry and away from God. Jezebel flaunted the debauchery and immorality by promoting Baal worship. Her behavior incensed the God of Creation. Elijah, however, was the exact opposite to Jezebel. He spoke truth about the living God with conviction. He constantly rebuked Jezebel and her husband for the use of their false gods. Elijah confronted Jezebel and had a contest with her evil prophets to prove the existence of the true and living God. "And call ye on the name of your gods, and I will call on the name of the Lord: and the God that answereth by fire, let him be God. And all the people answered as said, it is well spoken" (1 Kings 18:24).

The Baal prophets attempted to prove that their god was omnipresent but failed miserably as they made many futile attempts. They were not able to command the god Baal to let fire fall from the sky. In today's world it could be said they fizzled in their attempts to showcase Baal's power. It was then Elijah's time to prove God's sovereignty in the competition, and he had no doubt that God would deliver. Elijah made a plea to God for His presence, and his prayers were answered in a dramatic fashion. The Scripture proclaims: "Here me, O Lord, hear me, that this people may know that thou art the Lord God, and that thou hast turned their heart back again. Then the fire of the Lord fell, and consumed the burnt sacrifice, and the wood, and the stones, and the dust, and licked up the water that was in the trench" (1 Kings 18:37-38).

At the end of the competition, Elijah had all the prophets of Baal slain. The God of all creation reigned supreme in all His glory. The individuals who had witnessed God's work fell on their faces and worshipped Him. Elijah had proven with God's strength that there was only one true God. However, in the process, he had made an enemy of the Queen Jezebel. King Ahab reported the results of the competition to his wife Jezebel, and she was furious. Once she processed the news of the destruction of her god Baal, she threatened to take the life of Elijah. In a moment of weakness, Elijah became very afraid and fled to the mountain for the safety of his life.

Elijah became so distraught that he asked God to take away his life as he sat under a Juniper tree. In his moment of fragility, he mentioned to God that he alone could not defeat the enemy. God reminded him that he is never alone. In today's world, it could be said that Elijah's self-confidence was on shaky ground. In his moment of despair, God provided an angel to deliver food and drink for him on multiple occasions. The food which was delivered sustained him for forty days and forty nights. In Elijah's limitation, God afforded substance and prepared him for his journey ahead. He had Elijah written in the palm of His hands. In adversity and danger, God will always be there.

*****

Food for Thought: God is omnipresent. He will position people in places to pave your way. He will provide for you when the path appears rocky and is filled with obstacles. The path which you believe you should be on is not necessarily the one which is in God's plan. "So do not fear, for I am with you; do not be dismayed, for I am your God. I will strengthen you and help you; I will uphold you with my righteous right hand" (Isaiah 41:10 NIV).

Gratitude is Essential

Jamaican Proverb: "Cow neva know de use a him tail til him lose it"
Translation: Cow does not know the use of his tail until he loses it
Explanation: *Do not take things for granted or you do not know what you have until you lose it*

We are a fickle set of people, and we are often hard to please. It is either too cold, too hot, too wet, too dry, or too humid. I was blessed to have grown up on a Caribbean island with beautiful sunshine most of the year. However, I never appreciated the tropical sunshine until I experienced my first winter. I have lived in the Midwest and the Northeast, both regions known for cold weather. I recall a winter day in the Midwest in which it was relatively mild in temperature and presented with a slight wind. I thought it was a beautiful day. However, as I stood at the stop light waiting to cross the street, a lady who waited with me said, "Some weather, this wind is something else." I looked at her, and I smiled. "Well, I said it could be ten degrees below freezing and snowing." She looked at me shocked but smiled. My message had been delivered: Give thanks in all things.

Ungrateful Murmurs

The children of Israel reminded me of this lady at the stoplight. God directed Moses to lead them out of bondage in Egypt. They survived slavery and ten plagues, but they still found time to complain. They were guided by a pillar of light and a pillar of cloud. God delivered them across the Red Sea and drowned their pursuers. However, after all these marvelous works by God, it was met with grumblings. They continued complaining, this time about the lack of water. The Israelites continued drinking "the syrup of murmur." Nothing was ever good enough.

After their exhausting ordeal, one might surmise that the Israelites, who were supposedly tired and thirsty, would have been filled with gratitude. However, they complained to Moses about the lack of water. There was no doubt they were remembering the bounty of food and drink they left in Egypt. They were able to find water which was not fit for human consumption because it was bitter. The name of the place was called "Marah," meaning bitter. Once again, they made their dissatisfaction known to Moses. There was an intervention by God, and they were given instructions on how to prepare the water for drinking. After the continued display of God's greatness of delivering them from bondage, parting the Red Sea for their safe passage, destroying their captors, and providing a guidance directional system, the Israelites were complaining about water!

The Israelites were clothed in a layer of ungratefulness, their behavior was beyond belief.

The behavior of some individuals in today's world does not fall far from the pattern of the Israelites. We are often guilty of this display of daily ingratitude. Our lives are so consumed by materialistic gain that we lose focus of what is important. We race down the highways, oblivious of God in nature. We have no time to appreciate the birds chirping, the leaves waving, the rays of the sun, or the rainfall. There is food in the fridge, but we complain of being hungry; there are clothes in the closet, but we grumble of having nothing to wear. Our ingratitude is definitely comparable to the Israelites, who were consistent whiners. Instead of displaying hearts of gratefulness in thanksgiving, they were plagued with "spiritual amnesia."

The Israelites further complained of being hungry after their great rescue. God provided them with meat (quail) and bread (manna). However, it was still not enough. They kept complaining and turned to Idolatry by worshipping a golden calf. The behavior of the Israelites reminded me of a broken record; they just kept repeating the pattern of ingratitude. The Lord heard their cry and again gave Moses instructions of the impending provision of food and flesh for his people: "I have heard the murmurings of the of the children of Israel: speak unto them, saying, At even ye shall eat flesh, and in the morning ye shall be filled with bread; and ye shall know that I am the Lord your God" (Exodus 16:12). Although, God had made His appearance known many times, they were blinded by lack of appreciation.

Despite all God had done, they turned their backs on Him. There is a level of patience which is exhibited in every situation that is faced. God is patient and forgiving, but His mercy should not be taken for granted. He became angry at the children of Israel and their ungratefulness, and, as punishment, they were told a new generation would live to enter the promise land and all who came out of Egypt would die. The Israelites stayed on the incorrect side of the wilderness and their Creator for forty years because of complaining.

Gratitude is essential, and we should aspire to appreciate our storied memories and past blessings. If we forget past blessings, it may be compared to dishonoring God and His goodness. One memory which has stood the test of time and taught me a lesson in gratitude is the indelible mark which Hurricane Gilbert left on my life.

Frozen Gold

In September of 1988, Jamaica received an unwelcome visitor. It marched into our island at 130 miles per hour, causing mayhem and destruction. The visitor's name was Gilbert, Hurricane Gilbert if you please. It was labelled a category three hurricane. I was preparing to begin my fourth year of high school. This hurricane was a bit concerning to me as the fourth year of high school would lay the foundation for my final examinations. Gilbert had other ideas; it became a master of destruction as the storm wreaked havoc across my beloved island. Loose zinc sheets were seen flying across the roads. Massive tree branches stood limp in the face of mighty winds. Many of my neighbors watched with worried expressions and fear to see if their roofs would be next. I stood on the verandah and watched the awning strain against the winds. It was a scary yet fascinating experience viewing God's power.

At first, I enjoyed the novelty of not being in school. My classes were suspended for close to a month. This was before the internet, so we could not have virtual learning. However, the novelty soon wore off as I realized all the things that we were missing. There was no water, light, some food shortage, damaged property, and no friends. We were limited in the meals which we had because of the lack of power.

Canned corned beef (bully beef in the Jamaican vernacular) and cheese sandwiches became constant friends in my diet. However, my mother had some fresh pork which she seasoned to get it to a "corned" state prior to the storm. We enjoyed this treat of fried corned pork with ground provisions as it gave us a break from the sandwiches. Consequently, the one item I missed most was ice. My family and I began calling it "*Frozen Gold*."

There was no frozen gold in sight, and if you found it, the cost was at a premium. One of my mom's coworker stopped by our home after his shift ended. He was coming from a trip in the country, and he carried precious cargo: an Igloo with blocks of ice. You would have thought I had gotten one million dollars, ice never looked or tasted so good. My mother chipped the ice bricks into smaller pieces, placed the pieces in containers and delivered it to our neighbors along the avenue. I am forever grateful for ice cubes to this day. It is natural for us to be grateful for food, shelter, and clothing, but we often take for granted our bodily functions.

The Blessing of Bodily Functions

We are most often embarrassed of our bodily functions. Namely among them is flatulence. We become embarrassed whenever there is a need to "pass gas." Was it loud? Did they smell or hear it? We are so self-conscious. I grew to look forward to flatulence. I have had many surgeries in my lifetime, minor and major. God is the great physician, and I know He gives all the skills to the doctors on the surgical team. Whenever I would meet the surgical team, the most important person to me is the anesthesiologist. Once I meet the doctor, I like to inform them, "I know you hold my life in your hands with God's permission." However, it is the post-surgery visit from the surgeon that I found interesting. After they had checked the wound, vitals, diet, the question which often follows is, "Have you passed gas?"

Initially, when I did surgery and the surgeon asked this question, I laughed. However, there was a seriousness to the surgeon's face. If I did not "pass gas," I would not be getting discharged. Days after surgery, my focus was "passing gas." I thought it ironic that an action I was embarrassed about outside the hospital was now so vital for my well-being. When I did "pass gas," I was ever so grateful that I called it "The Sweet Perfume" for discharge. Nowadays, when I do "pass gas," I sometimes smile and remember my days laying in the hospital bed. This has given me the ability to always put things in perspective. Everything has a purpose and should be appreciated, even the sometimes embarrassing act of flatulence.

Dad and the Taxicab

Another memory comes to the forefront of my mind about flatulence and our attempt to cover this normal body function. As a child, I was my dad's shadow. We were inseparable like peas in a pod. My time with Dad was enjoyable. He was funny, loving, and kind. I was born at seven months premature and needed to have follow up visits to the hospital to monitor my progress. My dad was the designated parent who took me to my medical appointments, and he prepared accordingly. He packed lots of snacks, sandwiches, drinks, and fruits in our basket as we often spent hours at my appointments. It appeared that Dad was primed to feed an army instead of two people. One day, Dad and I took a taxicab to the hospital.

During the cab ride, a pungent odor enveloped the back seat of the car. The driver held a poker face and looked straight ahead, so did my Dad who was seated beside me. I asked him, "Dad, did you poop?" Dad barely acknowledged me and kept looking forward. I knew he was the one, so I blurted out with my four-year-old self, "Dad, talk di truth a yuh fart." The car exploded in laughter at the innocence of a child. I am betting my father was not thankful for my brutal honesty in that embarrassing moment.

What are you grateful for?

Who or what have you taken for granted?

*****

Food for Thought: "Half a bread is better than no bread!" I often hear this statement from my Mom and one of my close friends as it was a part of our local vernacular. It reminds me of the ability to look at perspectives in all cases. Gratitude should become ingrained in our spiritual DNA. As the apostle Paul proclaimed, "And having food and raiment let us be therewith content" (1 Timothy 6:8).

Truth in Love

Speak the truth and speak it ever
Cause it what it will
For he who hides the wrong he did
Does the wrong thing still?[1]

The absence of truth is the beginning of sorrows.

When we become governed by our emotions, we should be guided by a strong moral compass based on biblical principles. The Bible is considered one of the greatest books ever written. It tells of compassion, peace, grace, and judgement. Also, it gives us the ability to choose right from wrong. The choices that we have made recently have led to a major malfunction in the running of society. One glaring spot is the omission of truth. It appears individuals walk on eggshells in today's world because they do not wish to offend anyone.

Voice of Candor

In selected instances, the truth is sugar coated to hide the true meaning. Each day a new terminology is used to make an issue more acceptable to mainstream society. If someone tells a lie or a child has an argument with their par-

1 Research seemingly attributed the Poem to Henry William Dulcken 1832-1894

ent, reactions vary. The acceptable language is viewed as a child expressing themselves or that the person misspoke, and the "little" lie is not such a big deal. However, if someone chooses to voice their opinion based on their belief system in Jesus Christ, they are criticized and often called antiquated.

In various cases, individuals who speak their truth based on the Word of God are being accused of creating a hostile environment or being prudish. There are those individuals who are being muzzled or censored as they speak the fact. In a sense, the ability to speak straight forward and plain has been overshadowed by convoluted explanations. I reflect on Matthew 5:37, not in the aspect of saying "Yes" or "No" as an answer, but the simplicity and transparency of the retort. However, there are other instances, where individuals are accepting of this new concept as they do not wish to be viewed as "out of touch." Each time we take part in rationalizing these behaviors, we are assisting in the erosion of our moral fabric.

There are some instances where I question the voice of the objector in delivering the truth. Is their intent to harm or heal? Our language should always be laced with love and understanding. I recently heard of a situation where an unmarried young couple decided to move in together. The reason for moving in was not given, so I assumed it was a financial one. My initial response to my friend, "How could their parents condone this behavior?" My friend and I then realized we would hear the universal answer now given, "They are grown," "It's their life," or "I have to respect the rights of my child." We both gave our opinions with respect and ended the conversation as we each understood everyone has God given free will.

God has given us two wills: His permissive will and His perfect will. In the instance of the couple living together, the permissive will is blatantly evident. Many individuals have become distorters of the truth. In fact, there is no longer a shock value for certain behaviors or attitudes. We often think we are being respectful by giving individuals their space, but at what cost?

The Approach

I have been accused of being blunt in certain interactions. On occasion my approach can be discerned as cold. When I see an injustice or a perceived wrong, I become emotionally invested. At times when emotionally invested, I become impassioned. There are a selected group of my friends who will tell if I state, "Have you lost your damn mind?" signals I am not pleased with the situation. Was that the right approach? No. Do I get my point across? Sometimes. Jesus proclaims, "Sanctify them through thy truth: thy word is truth" (John 17:17). Christ's teachings were radical, and He constantly speaks the truth in love. Matthew 5:44 speaks to this radicalism which Jesus mentioned in telling us to love our enemies and bless those that curse us. That sentiment is often hard to process, but it exudes who Jesus is.

In your dispensing of the truth, you should strive to recognize love and wisdom as valued companions in your delivery.

Are you speaking the truth in love?

Do you "sugar coat" the truth to appease the masses?

*****

*Food for Thought***:** In some instances, the truth will not always be received well by others, but it must be said. It will feel at times like you are standing alone on a deserted island. However, when you speak the truth, God is by your side. The following scriptures acknowledge that the truth needs to be said: "But speaking the truth in love, may grow up into him in all things, which is the head, even Christ" (Ephesians 4:15). "He that speaketh truth speweth forth righteousness: but a false witness deceit" (Proverbs 12:17).

Changing World... Unchanging God

I often wonder what I would have done or who I would have been if I was born in another time period. Looking back at history, there are periods where my sentiments would have run the gamut. However, I have come to realize that God knows what we are able to deal with and the time in which we were placed. Like Queen Esther in the land of Persia, we are here in the twenty-first century for such a time as this period. Technology is faster, marriages are different, and truth and values have taken amnesic vacations. Marriage today carries a different meaning than that which was intended by God.

Marriage as God Intended

God created male and female and established what is known as the "Doctrine of Marriage." The biblical precepts state male and female become one and create new life: "So God created man in his own image, in the image of God created he him; male and female created he them. And God blessed them, and God said unto them, Be fruitful, and multiply, and replenish the earth, and subdue it: and have dominion over the fish of the sea, and over the fowl of the air, and over every living thing that moveth upon the earth" (Genesis 1:27-28).

Marriage is the foundation of society. If there is a shaking of the foundation, then values will crumble. God did not make man to be alone. He created a helping mate for Adam in the form of Eve. Male and female, He created them to complement each other. God thought so much of His creation that He took a body part of the male to form the female: "The man said, 'This is now bone of my bones and flesh of my flesh; she shall be called "woman," for she was taken out of man'" (Genesis 2:23 NIV).

Sexuality

When someone questions their sexuality, they are questioning God. He did not make a mistake in your creation. He knew you before you were formed in the womb (Jerimiah 1:5). He knows the number of hairs on your head (Luke 12:7). He knows your thoughts (Psalm 94:11). God knows all things; He loves His creations and wishes none to suffer. He often uses signs and warnings to gain our attention. One such sign is the rainbow. It is a covenant between God and man not to destroy the earth by water again. The rainbow shows God's promise to His people as a reminder (Genesis 9:8-17). However, in today's world, the colors connotate a different meaning. The rainbow colors are now a prominent symbol in the gay community. There are times when I surmise the original message of the rainbow will gradually fade from memory.

God made everything and says it is perfect. To question otherwise would be to call God a liar. In trying to replicate the doctrine of marriage in a same-sex manner, the world is saying God made a mistake. This is a fallacy as everything God does is done perfectly. He is not a man that He should lie, neither the son of man that He should say, "Whoops! I am sorry I have made a mistake." There is a manifestation of deception which has created a kind of fool's gold in crux. Statements such as "Love is love" or "You cannot help who you love" in relation to same-sex marriage parlays the idea that this partnership is as God intended. The world has become open to the concept of living as you are and being who you want to be. Consequently, creating what can be viewed as a realm of confusion.

A false sense of solace has been conceived. God created male and female. However, we are now faced with various terminologies such as pansexual, transgender, and non-binary, among others. In this time period, you realize that it is about God's permissive will not His perfect will. He will let the behavior continue until the stench overwhelms His spiritual nostrils.

The Concubine, the Levite, and His Host

There are many stories of sexual perversions throughout the Bible. The use of idolatry and violation of the body are prevalent. However, the story which I believe reflects the attitude which has permeated today's social structure in relation to sexuality takes place in the book of Judges, chapter 19. During that period, Israel was without a king, and it was everyone for their own accord. The story tells of a Levite and his concubine, who were on a journey, but it was difficult to find lodging. Concubines were accepted companions during this phase in time.

The Levite and his concubine met a man while searching for lodging. The man they encountered was a resident of the city. He begged the visitors not to remain in the streets as the hearts of men had gone vile. The man became their host and provided lodging in his home for the members of the group as was the custom of the day in the Middle East. Residents protected their visitors at all costs. As quickly as the party was sheltered within the doors of their host, the men of the city demanded to have the Levite so that they may have sex with him:

> Now as they were making their hearts merry, behold, the men of the city, certain sons of Belial, beset the house round about, and beat at the door, and spake to the master of the house, the old man, saying, Bring forth the man that came into thine house, that we may know him. And the man, the master of the house, went out unto them, and said unto them, Nay, my brethren, nay, I pray you, do not so wickedly; seeing that this man is come into mine house, do not this folly.
>
> Judges 19:22-23

The men of the city refused to listen to the master of the house. They were set in their wanton ways and wanted to have "fun." They were insistent in their bid to get the male visitor for pleasure. The host offered up his daughter and the concubine. The men accepted the offer of the concubine and violated her all night. Eventually, she died from the abuse of the men. In the morning, the Levite found the brutalized body of his concubine.

As I have reviewed this story, I realized that the society in which we live displays elements of the story. As with the men of the city, some individuals today will do what brings them pleasure. The master of the house and the Levite represents people who are aware that actions are wrong but support them anyway. Thereby, displaying a lack of moral convictions. Also, there was a lack of strong leadership as there was no king in Israel during the time of the assault. Selected members of the tribe of Benjamin perpetuated this sexual immorality. Similarly, the legality of same-sex marriage in the United States of America displayed a lack of respect for God's Word. The former President Barack Obama affirmed in 2015, when speaking from the Rose Garden on the same-sex marriage ruling, that the "Gay marriage ruling is a victory for America:"

> Our nation was founded on a bedrock principle that we are all created equal. The project of each generation is to bridge the meaning of those founding words with the realities of the changing times (Korte, "Obama").[2]

On June 26, 2015, the U.S. Supreme Court struck down all state bans on same-sex marriage, legalized it in all fifty states, and required states to honor out-of-state same-sex marriage licenses. God's Word is unchanging from one generation to the next. Same sex couples have the right to marry, and it is law. The times have become so mystified. Truth, lies, alternative facts, or maybe it is fool's gold.

[2] Korte, Gregory. "Obama: Gay marriage ruling is 'a victory for America.'" 26 June 2015. https://www.usatoday.com/story/news/politics/2015/06/26/obama-gay-marriage-ruling/29328755/

There are no flaws in God's creation, hence no room for confusion. The Apostle Paul advised in 1 Corinthians 14:33, "For God is not the author of confusion, but of peace, as in all churches of the saints." The issue of same sex marriage versus heterosexual marriage has filled the headlines of our electronic and printed media. Many have made their opinions known. However, the only opinion that matters is God's. He has the final say in all things. The Word of God never changes, and scripture admonishes us not to make changes. "Do not add to what I command you and do not subtract from it, but keep the commands of the Lord your God that I give you" (Deuteronomy 4:2 NIV).

*****

Food for Thought: My friend often states the ensuing, when confounded by decisions being made in society, "The one eye man is king in the land of the blind." In certain respects, it appears that the fear of the Lord has vanished, and there is a conforming to the times. We are in a changing world with an unchanging God.

How blinded have we become to the truth?

In the Blink of an Eye

> "To everything there is a season, and the time to every purpose under the heaven."
>
> Ecclesiastes 3:1

Time lost can never be regained!

Ask a dying man what he would do with an hour. Ask a child how they would treat another day with a dying parent. Ask an elite track athlete the value of seconds, or the expectant mother the span of nine months. Time dictates everything we do. When are you getting married? The age you should have kids. The exact age you should have enough money for retirement. The list is endless with many more scenarios. However, in all my years, I have never seen a timetable set for *When am I going serve God*? He allows us the freedom to live our lives. The will to choose is given freely to us. We constantly make our choices within His permissive will. However, what is our purpose on earth? How we spend our allotted time on earth leaves much to be desired.

Time's a Wastin'

During high school, my friends and I loved and respected each other, but we seldom used our time wisely. We spent many days congregating at our respective homes. Although highly capable, we occasionally completed the intended purpose of studying. Several days when we were together, there was no direct structure to our study plans. When we did study, we sometimes collapsed into giggles from one stupid joke or another. I vividly remember a particular day when Debbie and I decided to prepare for our accounting test. The incident in question could be viewed in retrospect as funny, but in the moment, I was terrified.

Debbie, the Area Leader, and Me

Debbie lived in an area that was controlled by an area leader. She was extremely focused on our accounting test preparation, and I needed her help. So, after school ended, instead of heading off with Rachel and Abigail, my destination this day was Debbie's home. We were busy laughing and talking about the events of the school day. Along the way, I got distracted and Debbie walked ahead of me into her community. I approached the community entrance, oblivious to everything as I was focused on getting to Debbie's house. Then I heard a booming voice, "A who yuh?" My interest captured, I snapped to immediate attention.

It was the area leader; this was the person who protected the residents of the community. I was frantically searching for Debbie, but she was far ahead of me. My one saving grace was that I was in uniform. So, without thinking, I blurted out my name and said, "I am going to Debbie's house for curry chicken back and boiled dumplings." There was not a thought or mention to our planned studying as it flew from my mind. The area leader paused and gave me a quizzical look as I responded to him. Realizing, I was not from the area, and that Debbie was indeed my friend, he burst out in laughter and said, "Awright yuh cool, enjoy di chicken back." There was no studying that day as I was a bit in shock from the greeting received. However, I did sit and enjoy some chicken back and dumplings with my friend and her family as it was being prepared upon our arrival. The lack of preparation for the exam should have been more frightening to me than the area leader, but it provided an outlet for me not to study. There were other days when we did study.

My friends and I did worry about our grades, and in that period, we applied ourselves and worked hard to get good grades. However, there were instances when we were minimally invested. We made time to visit Mr. Chin for his one-dollar beef patties. We cooked scrambled eggs, and other days, we steamed water crackers with fish gravy. The girls and I climbed the tamarind tree and enjoyed the sour fruit. We discussed a myriad of topics among us. There were days when Rachel would be my hair stylist as it was always in need of care. We enjoyed our days but never fully appreciated the value of our time in school.

The Power of If

My business teacher in high school would always say, "Ladies and Gentlemen one day you will say, 'If I had known,' *If* will be your biggest word." We heard her, but we really did not listen to her. Years later, I came to realize that she was spot-on. I often wonder how much more my friends and I would have accomplished if we had used our time more productively. Yet, despite not committing wholeheartedly to our schoolwork, we were adept at passing our examinations. I regretted that we wasted so much time in high school. However, my time in school, although not properly utilized academically, taught me valuable life lessons. These experiences have allowed me to cherish and invest wisely in the moments I now enjoy.

Have you ever wondered what you would do if you had a "Bank of Time"? Where you could make deposits, and when you needed time, you would make withdrawals to cover the perceived short fall of hours in your day. It is wishful thinking indeed, because that will never happen. God does not work on man's time but His own. 2 Peter 3:8 (NIV) best summarizes this sentiment: "But do not forget this one thing, dear friends: With the Lord a day is like a thousand years, and a thousand years are like a day." The world is changing at a rapid pace, and we should not sit and mourn the past but look to the investments we can make in the present to impact the future. Are you utilizing your time productively? You often think you will complete a task tomorrow or next week and not concentrate in the moment. Where and how you invest your time is paramount to your peace of mind.

Wasted Years

What if? The often-mentioned words for wasted years. When growing up, I knew of a man who was in a common law relationship with a woman for over two decades. They had eleven children together, and he was the sole provider. One evening, he was returning home from work, drunk. He was hit by a motor vehicle and killed. His common law wife and children were left shattered. Who would now be their provider? After his death, the family lived at the kindness of strangers and a small, allotted pension from the government. What wasted years! In hindsight, the biggest word in her vocabulary must have been "*if*." I wonder how many "ifs" have been used over the years. How often have you heard someone lament, "If I was only older"? The irony is you do not always appreciate the present moment, yet once you get to the desired older age, the new wish is to turn back the hands of time. I surmised Jacob wished Rachel were the younger of his uncle's daughters. His wish was not the reality of his situation, and so he was taught a valuable lesson in patience during his fourteen years of labor.

Jacob, Rachel, and Leah

I am not a scholar of the Bible, but the element of time fascinates me. Each story which is told can be viewed from the prospective of time. God created the earth in six days and rested on the seventh day. The children of Israel were in the wilderness for forty years. The flood lasted forty days. The Israelites were exiled for seventy years in Babylon. Warnings of three years of famine were given by the prophet Elijah. These are just a small collection of timely biblical events. However, the story of time which has left an impact is that of Jacob, Rachel, and Leah. This chapter of Jacob's life takes place in the book of Genesis, chapter 29.

Jacob went on a journey, and his destination led him to his uncle Laban, who had two daughters. Rachel, the younger sister, was considered a beauty. In today's world, she might be signed to be a fashion model. Leah, the oldest, was described to be not as fair as her younger sister. In our time, she might be referred to as "average" in appearance. Rachel was the first of the two sisters that was seen by Jacob. In current day society, we would say it was love at first sight for him. He was willing to complete the necessary task to make Rachel his wife.

As Jacob worked for Laban, he asked what his wages should be, and his uncle responded by asking what he thought should be the wages paid. Jacob responded in the following manner: "And Jacob loved Rachel; and said, I will serve thee seven years for Rachel thy younger daughter" (Genesis 29:18). The law of the land stated that the older daughter had to be married first. In order to accomplish this, Laban deceived Jacob into marrying Leah by omission and trickery. The deceiver Jacob was deceived. After realizing Laban's deception, Jacob worked an additional seven years for the hand of Rachel. So, in essence, Jacob toiled a mind boggling fourteen years to get the bride of his choice. I respected Jacob's perseverance in working towards what he wanted, despite being deceived. This sign of dedication to a cause is a valued commodity.

> *Do you give up on a situation before there is a breakthrough?*
>
> *How often have you walked away from a task because it was not done in the manner you envisioned?*

*****

Food for Thought: Perseverance and time are good bed fellows. God is always on time in our lives even though the time for deliverance seems never-ending. As a friend once said, "Any day above ground is a good day." So, we should strive to use time wisely as tomorrow is promised to no one. Our time should be governed by the phrase "God willing" in all plans we make.

Obedience

> But this thing commanded I them, saying, Obey my voice, I will be your God, and ye shall be my people: and walk ye in all the ways that I have commanded you, that it may be well unto you.
>
> Jeremiah 7:23

The Embarrassment of Disobedience

Obedience is one of the hardest virtues to fulfill, especially if you are a teenager. In that stage of development, you believe you know everything, you feel invincible, and rebellion is visible in some situations. There were a few times when I would go against advice given by Mom. I vividly remember one such incident. My dad lived abroad, and he had great taste in clothing. He supplied me with all the current fashions of the day. On one occasion, he sent me a hobble dress which I adored. It was long, below the knee, purple and black, buttons on the front of the dress, and belted at the waist. This dress was my pride and joy as it was form fitting.

Mom looked at my outfit after I had finished getting dressed and told me to loosen some of the buttons below the knee. She predicted the buttons would be broken if I wore it with all the buttons being fastened. I boldly told her, "No!" I further voiced to her I knew how to walk in the heels, and the buttons would be fine. My mother was to be proven a prophet.

I approached the bus stop walking like I was strutting down the runway during New York fashion week. The bus was approaching earlier than expected. Well, what a dilemma I faced. I did not envision myself running in the dress. I needed to get to church on time as I hated being late. I ran as my life depended on it. Can you envision what happened next? I heard the buttons popping, I lost two before I got to the bus step. I walked gingerly to church to avoid exposing my legs, as I had lost three buttons in total. When I got home, I did not wish to tell my mother about my buttons, but I did. Ever the diplomat, she never said, "I told you so." She took the dress and replaced the buttons. If I had not been so stubborn, my dress would not have been damaged. I would not have had suffer being exposed and embarrassment. There is a consequence to every choice and decision we make in our daily lives.

There are many cases of obedience/disobedience to God in the Bible. The story of Jonah being instructed to minister to the people of Nineveh, and Isiah walking nude to prove a point to Judah at God's request, is quite revealing. Both men travelled different paths in acquiescing in the department of compliance to God's mandate.

Jonah on a Mission

God gave Jonah a mandate to speak to the people of Nineveh. Sin was running rampant, and the people of the city had departed from God. Jonah did not want to help the people of Nineveh. In fact, he believed they should suffer and decided to disobey God's given order.

> But Jonah rose up to flee unto Tarshish from the presence of the Lord, and went down to Joppa; and he found a ship going to Tarshish: so he paid the fare thereof, and went down into it, to go with them unto Tarshish from the presence of the Lord. But the Lord sent out a great wind into the sea, and there was a mighty tempest in the sea, so that the ship was like to be broken.
>
> Jonah 1:3-4

Jonah defied God and tried to hide from the assignment and God's presence. The fact is we cannot hide from God. Psalm 139:8-9 explains that God will find you even in the depths of Hell or the utter most parts of the sea. Jonah learned a hard lesson and received a harsh punishment. He was asleep in the sides of the ship, and the sailors pleaded with him so they could avoid God's wrath. Jonah explained to them who he was and the fact that he was running from the presence of God. The sailors became afraid as the ship threatened to break in half from the storm. Knowing he was the cause of the impending destruction, he asked to be thrown overboard.

Once overboard, he was swallowed by a fish which was provided by God. Jonah remained within the belly of the fish for three days and three nights. He was eventually released from the fish after praying from its belly. He asked God to be forgiven for his disobedience. The Lord replied by communing with the fish, and he vomited Jonah out on land. What an awesome God! He communicated with the fish! Despite Jonah's disobedience, God kept him safe in the belly of the fish.

Jonah had his initial mission of ministering to the residents of Nineveh to complete. Likewise, God will have us complete our divine assignment by any means necessary. "Go to the great city of Nineveh and proclaim to it the message I give you" (Jonah 3:2 NIV). So, Jonah arose and did what he was supposed to do from the beginning. He delivered God's message to the people of Nineveh, who repented. This showed the level of God's mercy and grace in the face of disobedience.

> *What if you responded to God the first time he asked you to complete a task?*
>
> *How many of you are "Jonahs" of your time?*

Isaiah Exposed

Isaiah is considered as one of the greatest prophets in the Bible. He responded to his calling and began his ministry a few years before King Uzziah died. Isaiah performed many great acts on behalf of God. Although many people ignored his message, he persevered in his ministry. Isaiah was asked by God to show the prophecy against Egypt and Ethiopia and deliver a message to Judah—how remarkable. God commanded Isaiah, and he dutifully obeyed:

> At the same time spake the Lord by Isaiah the son of Amoz, saying, Go and loose the sackcloth from off thy loins, and put off thy shoe from thy feet. And he did so, walking naked and barefoot. And the Lord said, Like as my servant Isaiah hath walked naked and barefoot three years for a sign and wonder upon Egypt and upon Ethiopia.
>
> Isaiah 20:2-3

What!

Did the Scripture say that Isiah walked naked for three years? That must have been a humiliating experience for him. However, he obeyed God because he knew God would never ask him to do something wrong. He was being used in a manner which reflected God's love. In essence, what his obedience did was have the people realize the lengths God would go to get His message delivered. He valued their salvation greatly.

Can you imagine pastors of today being told by God as an act of obedience they should walk naked for three years to convince the people of His love for them? That would not be happening in today's world. We have evolved into an appearance-conscious system and often worry what others think of us. Also, from a legal perspective, it would be considered indecent exposure. Our times have changed, and therefore, we must adapt our ministry methods. However, in the end, only what we do for Christ will stand the test of time. He gives us our assignments, but He will never leave our sides. How we respond to the instructions given will dictate our paths.

What extent are you willing to be uncomfortable for the Gospel of Jesus Christ?

*****

Food for Thought: You often pay a steep price when you are disobedient as there is a consequence for every choice we make. However, there is always a blessing in being obedient to God. The Scripture reminds us that disobedience is as the sin of sorcery, and stubbornness comparable to impudence.

Divine Institution

"Therefore, shall a man leave his father and his mother, and shall cleave unto his wife: and they shall be one flesh."
Genesis 2:24

There are many Bible stories which bring awe, joy, and reverence, while other stories bring anger and confusion. The story of Hosea and Gomer brings forth the latter emotions upon face value. Their relationship reflects God's love for Israel even in their rebellious state. God mandated Hosea to accomplish a task which would be unheard of in today's world. He was to marry an adulteress per God's command. The understanding of cheating spouses is incomprehensible, trust once broken will be difficult to re-establish.

The celebrity and media culture which drives our world displays marriages where partners enter and exit their unions as if in child's play. The idea of getting to know a partner or avoiding outside destructive influences is not often considered. In some instances, marriages today have been turned into a public spectacle and romanticized. The work needed to make relationships succeed is glossed over. Marriage should not be entertainment or a band-aid that will fix prior ailments.

One Flesh

Marriage is a sacred bond between a man and a woman, as per biblical precepts. It is a union where two biblically become one. The partnership should represent love and respect. God refers to His relationship with the church as a marriage. However, recent cracks have become visible in the partnership God ordained. Opinions differ on adultery. Some believe work on the marriage, others say leave the marriage, and the remainder are neutral. Viewpoints notwithstanding, individuals should pursue counseling and aspire to offer forgiveness. Christ instructed Peter when he asked about forgiveness of your fellow man to approach in this manner, "I say not unto thee until seven times: but until seventy times seven" (Matthew 18:22). The figurative number of four hundred and ninety stresses the importance of reconciliation.

The fact that no one is perfect, and we all make mistakes, should govern our relational decisions. Certain individuals choose to remarry, while for others there is no clear path to fixing the relationship. Many second chances have proven to be successful. I am not a theologian, but my interpretation of the scriptures which speaks to the topic of divorce is that marriage is permanent. If it is dissolved, adultery is the one clear reason I can find given for divorce within the Word of God.

Godly Instructions

- "Wherefore they are no more twain, but one flesh. What therefore God had joined together let no man put asunder" (Matthew 19:6).

- "It had been said, Whosoever shall put away his wife, let him give her a writing of divorcement. but I say unto you, that whosoever shall put away his wife, saving for the cause of fornication, causeth her to commit adultery: And whosever shall marry her that is divorced committeth adultery" (Matthew 5:31-32).
- "For the woman which hath a husband is bound by the law to her husband so long as he liveth; but if the husband be dead, she is loosed from the law of her husband. So then if, while her husband liveth, she be married to another man, she shall be called an adulteress: but if her husband be dead, she is free from the law; so that she is no adulteress, though she be married to another man" (Romans 7:2-3).
- "Jesus replied, Moses permitted you to divorce your wives because your hearts were hard. But it was not this way from the beginning" (Matthew 19:8 NIV).

Voices of Concern

I hear the voices resonating with concern:

- What if there is a need for companionship?
- Should individuals remain single after a divorce?
- What if a spouse has cheated?
- If someone is remarried, and their first spouse is alive, are they committing adultery?
- What if you realized you made a mistake by entering this marriage?

- These instructions do not apply today as they are outdated.

All valid questions and statements. Consequently, the only answer I can give is this, live by the direction of the Bible. Trust God, that He will direct you to make the right decision as each person has to give a retort for all their actions in account to God.

Cautionary Input, Warnings, and Intrusions

I believe some couples are warned before entering matrimony. However, these signs are often ignored, not seen, or there is a choice not to see the signs. I have witnessed many situations where signs have been ignored. In most cases, the prevailing warning cry is always the same, "Wait, give the relationship time to grow." The care shown by concerned parties is often rebuffed. The result of ignoring the warnings have often ended in a stream of regretful tears for the parties involved.

Individuals typically do not temper their expectations of marriage and at times allow interfering outside influences to bolster these hopes. When a perceived expectation is not met, it creates a level of regret. This discontent fosters an unhealthy home environment between the spouses. Friends and family are at times the root causes for such upheavals. However, there are instances where the couples have not done their due diligence toward their perspective partner. They have not acquired the one opinion that matters by seeking God in prayer. Also, individuals should probe their respective relationships. This is not to infer that their lives should be dissected as trust is important. However, if there is a powerful inclination of doubt, do not ignore it. In conjunction with God's help, trust that still small voice.

An acquaintance of mine was planning to get married. She was excited to begin this new chapter in her life, and I was happy for her. I ventured to ask questions of my colleague about her perspective spouse. The questions were a mixture of basic and background information. She was not able to answer select questions about him. My queries and her lack of answers were not well received and made for an uncomfortable moment. I walked away from the conversation praying that their relationship would succeed.

I remember being a classic example of an outside influence which could be construed as destructive. A friend was dealing with a cheating spouse, called and requested my opinion. My response to that individual was swift, "Leave the relationship." I offered no outlet for prayer or seeking Godly counsel. The reaction I gave was from a place of anger and hurt for my friend. There was no thought given to the devastating effect which my response could have created by possibly further compounding the issue.

God should be an important part of the discussion in the testing times in a relationship. My mother once said, "A broken engagement is easier than a broken marriage." In essence, stop the heart break before it happens. However, if the marriage is already established, involve God in your decisions and work on making the union succeed.

Hosea and God's Everlasting Love

Having said all that, let us examine Hosea, whose name means salvation. He had no outside interference or noted cautionary tale from family or friends. He was commanded by God to marry a known adulteress. This was a mandate he would not ignore as he understood that it was representational to minister to the lost children of Israel as he would his wife Gomer. Think of a little child that keeps repeating the same mistake over and over; the parent is patient with that child and shows love and understanding. Likewise, God will go to any lengths to get our attention. In this case, Hosea was given the onerous task to minister to Israel.

Would you have obeyed God's command to marry someone of disrepute?

You will never know everything about someone. People will change after marriage as it is a learning and maturation process. However, there are critical topics which should be addressed prior to marriage. There should be a certainty that you and your partner share common ground. This common ground may manifest itself in the topics such as spiritual, financial, emotional, and social interest.

When God's command was issued, the criteria for Hosea's marriage was not typical. Gomer was not from a reputable family nor had a respectable profession. She was the emblematic channel God needed to bring Israel back to Him. Gomer constantly cheated on Hosea, and each time she was unfaithful, he brought her back home. I am not aware of many individuals who would continuously love or tolerate a cheating spouse as it wears on the emotions. "Then said the Lord unto me, Go yet, love a woman beloved of her friend, yet an adulteress, according to the love of the Lord towards the children of Israel, who look to other gods and love flagons of wine" (Hosea 3:1).

Consequently, Hosea loved Gomer with an everlasting love. Likewise, God loved Israel in a similar fashion. He wanted them saved although they rejected him and lived in a life of debauchery and idolatry. God's grace and mercy abounded towards His people. Gomer and Hosea's relationship can be looked at from two perspectives. A man's love for his wife, no matter the circumstance, and God's love for His people. In a sense, both the physical and spiritual adultery are betrayals. However, in both instances the unifier was love.

*****

Food for Thought: Love will cover many of our sins. As humans, we are prone to making mistakes, and healing broken relationships takes time. Marriage takes effort and compromise from both parties as it is a covenant between partners and God. "Therefore, turn thou to thy God: keep mercy and judgement and wait on thy God continually" (Hosea 12:6). The command from God to Hosea appears harsh, but it highlights the depths He would go to secure our love and obedience. Also, it emphasizes God's feelings of disappointment when we stray from His Word.

Shades of Grey
By Mindy Tucker

What a day
What a drama
Signs of the time, the great dilemma
We are in a time and place where yeah means nay
Happy no longer means gay
That's because we are living in shades of grey
Compromise solidifies the foundation
As honesty and trust are left grasping for survival
Where are You on this color wheel?
Are you painting in color or shades of grey?
We are numb when a young life is lost
When a junkie pushes the needed there
is no longer an alarm caused
That's because we are painting in shades of grey
Gangs are the families
Dons are the daddies
Innocence lost in shades of grey
Discipline and respect a lost way of life
You know its dread when expletives flow
from the palette instead of praise

That's because we are surrounded by shades of grey
We are the voice that's gone silent
There's an urgency to become the force we once were
We need, to sit greet and meet again:
Truth moral values, love, respect and patience
We need to seek and save the lost
We need to break the hold at all cost
Shades of grey?
Yeah Right!
Not when Christ blood ran red
He came for a purpose to erase the wheel of hatred
Shades of Grey no more
When our sins on the cross he bore
Where are you on this color wheel?
This canvas called life
Are you painting in color or shades of grey?

The Prodigal Effect

A Modern Version of the Prodigal Son (*Luke 15:11-32*)

A multimillionaire has two sons which he adores with all his heart. The older son is diligent, attentive, and respects his father. The younger son believes he is invincible, entitled, and thinks he knows everything. Prior to his age to collect his inheritance, he approaches his father with his lawyers asking for his share of his father's wealth. The father, although not believing he is ready for such a large sum of money, gives him the amount he demanded. He knew his son was strong willed and would use whatever means necessary to get his inheritance.

The elder brother, seeing this display of disrespect, becomes upset at the situation. In the long run, the younger brother squanders his money and returns home hoping to be servant. His Father greets him with open arms and has a five-star banquet with music and dancing in his tribute. The older son returns from a day in the board room and becomes furious at his father for neglecting his diligence. Although, this is a modern retelling of Luke 15:11-32, it is a mirrored reflection of the parable told by Jesus in biblical times.

A Mixture of the Old and New

Why did the father welcome the younger son with open arms? The grace and mercy he dispensed was commendable. He forgave him, although the younger son's behavior was detestable. The story often confounds many because of the father's response. In the biblical version and the modern version, all exudes a level of privilege and disrespect on the younger son's side. The lack of planning and the notorious and irreverent living were all plain to see. The youngest sibling made a reckless choice and lived like there was no tomorrow. His father acquiesced to his request and gave him his portion of the inheritance although it broke his heart. In essence, letting him live his life to his liking. The older son was disheartened by his father's response to his brother's return. However, he could not undermine the tradition. The inheritance was his money to have by right. Likewise, today we often hear the statements, "It is their life" or "They have the right." Independence is valid, the ability to make wise choices and decisions are welcomed. However, the younger son's decision to squander his inheritance fell short of a wise choice.

Leaving a Reckless Life

The younger brother enjoyed a life of revelry. When his inheritance was all spent and all his "friends" had left him, the younger son was a broken man. He turned to the only job he was able to get, feeding the pigs. He was made to feel like he had eaten a slice of "Humble Pie." He realized what a massive mess he had made of his life. I surmised that, as he sat eating the pig's food, smelled the stench of the filth and mud in the pig pen, saw the swarming flies in the heat of the day, he was prompted to make a choice.

He examined his diminished stature and arrived at the conclusion to return home as a servant in the splendor of his father's mansion. I envisioned he collected what was left of his meager and tattered belongings with calloused hands and headed to his father's house. He was a humbled and shattered son who was brought low to his knees. His broken-hearted father saw him approaching and ran to greet him. A party was arranged in honor of the younger son, despite his irresponsible behavior.

The older brother was a model of responsibility and the dutiful son. He chose to remain with his father and work in the fields. He asked for no privileges in his honor. As he returned from a day of work in the fields, he heard a celebration happening in the mansion. One may surmise he would have been sweaty, tired, and thirsty from work. He heard the celebration was for his long-lost brother, and he became irate. This type of festivity for his brother's behavior could be equivalent to someone being rewarded for failing their exams or crashing the family car.

After a hard day of labor, this was not the news the older brother wanted to hear. He felt justified in his anger towards his brother. One may infer he felt underappreciated by his father. He articulated this sentiment, "Lo, these many years I have served thee, neither transgressed I at any time thy commandment: and yet thou never gavest me a kid, that I might make merry with my friends" (Luke 15:29). It could be said that the older brother was in a conflicted state of mind.

There have been times in life when we have all responded like the older brother. It is often disheartening when you have done all you can to achieve a goal but fall short. Yet, you see others who have disregarded the Word of God being elevated in life. However, the scripture tells us, "I have been young and now I am old; yet have I not seen the righteous forsaken nor his seed begging bread" (Psalm 37:25). If some of us were in the field with the dutiful brother, we might have shared his emotions. It is in that moment that we let our flesh control our thoughts and actions.

> *What if God interacted with mankind in the manner which our actions and thoughts dictated?*

It would be a world most sorrowful. God is not like man; mercy is dispensed freely when asked as He wishes that no soul be excluded from His Kingdom. The father in the parable loved both his sons and was able to give a measure of understanding and grace equally to each brother. The father's behavior of fairness mirrors the owner of the vineyard as he went to seek daily workers.

The Generous CEO (*Matthew 20:1-16*)

The scripture tells us about the owner of a property who goes looking for workers to toil in his vineyard. He made several recruitment trips at multiple points throughout the day. One could compare him to the recruiter from the Human Resource Department. His contracted agreement with each person was a penny notwithstanding the hour in which they started. At the end of the day, as he paid the workers for their labor, each received a penny as agreed. There were grumblings among the earlier workers about receiving the same pay as later workers.

This scenario would be akin to someone working in an organization for ten years and making thirty dollars per hour. Then, an individual recently graduated from college with no experience ends up making the same amount of money. In today's world, there would be lawsuits for bias, and in some instances, the unions would get involved. However, the owner did not break his contract with the workers. He paid the agreed sum of money to each worker. The boss's response to the laborers' murmurs would have caused initial chaos in today's world. He voiced the following to his workers: "Friend, I do thee no wrong: didst not thou agree with me for a penny?" (Matthew 20:13). He implored the disgruntled workers that they were paid fairly, according to their verbal contract. The above-mentioned scenarios brought about an introspective mindset, and I wondered the following:

> *Have you ever been in a position where someone got a promotion which you believed you should have gotten?*
>
> *How well do you handle perceived slights?*
>
> *Is your first reaction to punish or forgive someone?*

*****

*Food for Thought***:** The message of the perceived injustices in both cases is mercy and fairness for mankind. None of us are worthy of the gift of eternal life. It is only by God's grace that we can dine at His table. The father's response to his oldest son's charge of injustice was priceless. In essence, he was saying it is greater to forgive than hold a grudge, or you, too, will become lost. We should always strive to choose joy over bitterness. The perception that someone has been slighted or forgotten in certain cases is a sign of God's built-in protection for your life. In essence, you are where you ought to be, not where you think you should be.

You Are More Than

"So, God created man in his own image in
the image of God created he him..."

Genesis 1:27

The subject of low self-esteem has become a major talking point in today's world. This lack of self-confidence has encumbered many lives. When you expose your life to self-scrutiny, your flaws become amplified, and you sometimes drown yourself in self-pity. Our aspirational lists are viewed by the societal standards for beauty and excelling. However, the idea of low self-esteem is not a new concept to mankind. In biblical times, we are aware of two individuals embodied in Gedeon and Moses, who suffered from various forms of self-doubt. This condition often manifests itself into depression, inadequacy, self-criticism, anger, and anxiety, to list a few. These diabolic forces permeate our lives and swindle us of our peace, positivity, and hope.

Gedeon

Gedeon complained to God that he was not from the right family. In fact, he said of all his father's children, his significance to his family was minimal—not realizing the gifts which God had poured inside of him. He expounded to

God: "Oh, my Lord, wherewith shall I save Israel? Behold my family is poor in Manasseh, and I am the least in my father's house" (Judges 6:15). Gedeon was slow to believe that God would give him the victory over the Midianites.

Self-doubt consumed Gedeon, making him question his abilities. The Midianites were great in number, and Gedeon was fearful that his army would not be strong or numbered enough to win the battle. God disagreed with Gedeon. In fact, He thought that his army was too large. So, God instructed Gedeon to select his men for battle. At the end of the selection process, Gedeon was left with three hundred men in his army, far less than the thousands of men that served on the opposing Midianite side. God was proving to Gedeon that His strength would be enough to defeat the Midianites. Gedeon obeyed God's directions, and he was indeed victorious.

God replied to Gedeon's plea of perceived inadequacy:

- "And it came to pass the same night, that the Lord said unto him. Arise, get thee down unto the host; for I have delivered it into thine hand" (Judges 7:9).
- "And the Lord said unto him, Surely I will be with thee, and thou shalt smite the Midianites as one man" (Judges 6:16).

Gedeon went on to do great things for God as Israel's fifth Judge. He was a highly skilled military strategist, who employed the aspect of surprise in his attacks and defeated the Midianite Army. Gedeon's temperament was aligned in such a manner that, once he was convinced of a feat, he was able to act on his beliefs. Although, he initially questioned God and His instructions, he was able to destroy his family's idols. Thereby, displaying his faith in God. This activation of faith gained him an installment in the exclusive Hall of Faith in Hebrews 11.

Moses

Although Moses once lived in the palace of Pharaoh, he had escaped Egypt because he killed a man in anger. God had plans for Moses, despite his sordid past. He was chosen by God to liberate His people from Egypt, despite his label as a killer and a perceived weakness of a speech impediment. However, despite God's stamp of approval, Moses was not confident in his ability to convince the Egyptians and appear in Pharaoh's court. "And Moses answered and said, But, behold, they will not believe me, nor harken unto my voice: for they will say, the Lord hath not appeared unto thee" (Exodus 4:1).

The Lord replied to Moses defense of alleged insufficiency:

While explaining to God that he was inadequate, he held a rod in his hand. God used the rod to prove the point that He would be with Moses as he performed great works. Moses was surprised at the miraculous act God performed, yet he still had self-doubt. One might surmise he was unwilling to change his viewpoint. "And He said, Cast it on the ground. And he cast it on the ground, and it became a serpent and Moses fled from before it. And the Lord said unto Moses, Put forth thine hand and take it by the tail. And he put forth his hand and caught it, and became a rod in his hand" (Exodus 4:3-4).

Moses had an "Anyone but Me Mentality" as he constantly threw roadblocks in front of God about his ability and lineage. At times, his distractions made God angry, but God prevailed in getting his attention. Moses presented his case before God in a manner which appeared to be a rock-solid case for being excused from his task assigned. He highlighted his less than impressive credentials to appear before the Pharaoh and highlighted his speech impairment. He proclaimed:

- "And Moses said unto God, Who am I that I should go unto Pharaoh, that I should bring forth the children of Israel out of Egypt?" (Exodus 3:11).
- "And Moses said unto the Lord, O my Lord I am not eloquent neither heretofore, nor since thou has spoken unto they servant: but I am slow of speech and of a slow tongue" (Exodus 4:10).

The Lord responded to Moses roadblocks and gave assurances:

- "And the Lord said unto him, Who hath made man's mouth, or who maketh the dumb, or deaf, or the seeing, or the blind? Have not I the Lord?" (Exodus 4:11).
- "And God said unto him, Certainly I will be with thee; and this shall be a token unto thee, that I have sent thee" (Exodus 3:12).

Despite the roadblocks created by Moses, God delivered an answer each time. Moses was used mightily by God. He completed the task of leading the Exodus of the Israelites from Egypt. Moses recorded the Ten Commandments, became a great author writing the first five books of the Bible (The Pentateuch), and left a legacy for Joshua to build on. Also, he was installed in the Hall of Faith in Hebrews 11, despite his perceived inadequacy.

Performing in My Own Strength

These scenarios replicate earth runnings in today's world. I am not tall enough; I have a stutter; I am too fat; I am too thin, or I am too tall, have all been uttered in one form or another from our self-doubting lips. Life can be intimidating, and I can understand the fear of rejection and failure. However, when we operate within our own strength, we are making room for the tentacles of fear. God designed us to be fearless and lean on Him in times of doubt. "For God has not given us a spirit of fear, but of power, and of love, and of a sound mind" (2 Timothy 1:7).

During high school, I remember being chosen to represent my colleagues in a teen program called *"Rapping."* It was a new television series on the scene for young people which explored the current and social topics of the day. One of my English teachers thought I would be a good delegate to speak on behalf of my high school in this media. Her reasoning was that I often represented them in drama festivals and would have been comfortable on stage. I had no experience working in this forum. I attended the taping, despite not feeling confident, but thinking I would get it done somehow. How different could being in a studio be versus the stage? For luck I "borrowed" my brother's t-shirt without his knowledge and trusted that he would not see the airing of the program.

At the top of the program, I introduced myself to the studio audience—after which, I experienced a "brain fart" and froze like a deer in headlights. I sat muted for the duration of the taping. Days after the airing of the program, my friends wondered why I had sat silently in the studio. I had no answers to their questions as I was still wondering why I froze. Apparently, the t-shirt was not so lucky after all. Did this mean that I was not a good public speaker? Far from it.

I disappointed myself, my teacher, and colleagues and let the fear of failing paralyze me in front of the cameras. A major lack of self-confidence and doubt had taken control as I had forgotten that I work in God's strength, not my own. This was a costly reminder to get on a nationally televised program. It was a chastening experience.

*****

Food for Thought: Remember, you are made in God's image. As an heir in the bloodline of Christ, be encouraged and strong in the knowledge of your innate power. So, as God was with Moses and Gedeon, so, too, is He with you. God will magnify your gifts for His service, so do not get caught in the net of self-doubt. "For I the Lord thy God will hold thy right hand, saying unto thee, Fear not; I will help thee" (Isaiah 41:13).

The Heritage

> "Train up a child in the way he should go: when he is old, he will not depart from it."
>
> Proverbs 22:6

We have often heard this verse of scripture quoted in one form or another. I believe it is a road map for individuals who care for children. I infer many individuals have taken this to heart. We should consider this a mandate as children are on loan to us. In essence, we are the earthly guardians of the children we are blessed with, and we will answer to God about how we cared for them. Consequently, the seeds we have planted and nurtured will dictate the ideals which are harvested. There are many circumstances where the time and love invested does not provide the desired result. However, once you have done your noblest, then you have done enough. However, there will be a selected number of adults that have not shouldered their responsibilities.

The Village

I believe children are our greatest assets, yet some parents spend more time with their stock portfolios than they do with their children. We should treat children as being in a contractual relationship with God. Whether we are biological parents, family, or working in a capacity with children, it is our job to honor the contents of that contract. We have failed them miserably in certain respects. An African proverb declares, "It takes a village to raise a child." If that proverb is true, then there are some residents in villages that have shirked their responsibilities. I believe, as adults, we have enabled some children as they find it hard to function outside of the realm of gadgets. There are instances where, instead of standing by the rules which they have established, some adults get manipulated as there is an emotional tug towards the child complaining of the perceived difficulty of their homework. Consequently, some children state that they need a break after minimal effort is given towards the schoolwork. To an extent, some adults have chosen the path of least resistance with this "break" as investing time or exploring other avenues with the child is sometimes viewed as time-consuming. This "break" in many cases is an opportunity to use an electronic gadget, hence the enabling. Select parents are now friends with an aim to please their child. Are you as a member of the village to blame?

Dropping the Proverbial Ball

A few years ago, I had a conversation with a teenager. She had threatened to run away from home. The reason, her mother had taken her cellular telephone away. I sat with a neutral expression on my face, showing no judgement. My training allowed me to empathize with her as I realized the phone represented a lifeline to some teenagers, and they dealt with many stressors. However, my practical side was screaming, "What in the world!" I saw this action as a form of manipulation as I was vaguely familiar with the dynamics of their relationship.

I listened to the teenager's side of the story and offered support, empathy, and some realistic feedback. My practical side was having a difficult time processing the episode. Why was she threatening to run away? Because her cellular phone was taken away by her mother? The mother that has worked hard to pay for the phone? I surmised it was an attempt by her mom to discipline the teenager. However, I wondered what the child was trying to say to her mother in her state of anguish as this was not typical behavior.

We are occasionally guilty of codling our children. Teachable moments during occasions of mistakes, mishaps, despair, or deceit are not adequately addressed. Investing times of empathy and room for sharing are not often employed. The bonds of trust between some adults and their children have not been fortified. The raising of our children has been left to technology; it is an advancement that has enhanced our lives in many positive ways, but also a detriment in many ways to our children. However, innovations and advancements which are made in technology reflect in the behavior patterns of our children.

Several children are no longer able to reason, analyze, and cope with challenging situations or interact personally in social situations. I often wonder how two children could be in the same room, sitting next to each other, and conversing by texting. This type of behavior is quickly becoming the normal way of communicating. Chosen solutions by some children have reflected poorly on adult leadership. These communication solutions are the outlets which enhances the child's inability to express themselves outside the realm of emojis or hyphenated text as some adults have not invested the time in the child's development. As followers of Christ, we are meant to be different. God should be in our interactions with our children.

I am not saying all children fall into such a category in communicating, but for the most part, we have enabled or ignored these behaviors as "attention seeking." We are then left to control the two-headed monster which has been created because of our lack of investment. It is fascinating to note that, in some cases, there is more respect for our material possessions than for our children.

Would you leave the care of your brand-new car to an architect?

Would the plumber be able to fix the electrical wiring in your house?

Yet, we have left what I deem as our most precious commodity to the whims of technology. They draw their knowledge from various websites as we frantically go about our day to provide for the household. In other cases, we become annoyed when dealing with the children. This behavioral pattern by adults affects the children mentally and emotionally as some develop a lack of self-love or low self-esteem. Different times and approaches to child rearing today you say, but God never changes. "For I am the Lord I change not" (Malachi 3:6).

Kryptonite Power of No!

I often hear the saying "As goes the child so goes society." Given the current state of our value system, I would say someone has dropped the proverbial ball. I recently sat at an airport departure gate awaiting my flight. A group of individuals, that appeared to be a family of six, entered and sat down. The father decided to seek breakfast for members of the family along with three of his children. Below is an excerpt from the conversation between mother and child that were left at the gate. The child did not appear to be older than four years of age. The female child begins to cry.

Mother: Honey what is it?
Child: (Mumbles to her mother about wanting to go with her father as he seeks breakfast for the family).
Mother: No
Child: (Throws herself on the floor and continues crying)

(Father returns to the gate upon hearing the child crying and seeks to find the reason for the outbursts)

Father: Is everything okay?
Mother: You know how she gets when you tell her, "No!"

I examined the prevailing circumstances. Traveling in today's world by yourself is an ordeal, let alone with a family of six. I considered the following factors: A young child, early morning travel, the child might have been hungry, or she wanted to go with her father. It could have been any number of issues. However, the mother's last statement started me thinking. I realized that select children and teenagers are not receptive to the word "No." This lack of reception has created a plethora of problems. As kryptonite is to the fictional character Superman, so is the word "*No*" to some of today's children.

Parents have overextended themselves for some children, who have no appreciation for money. Who gives an expensive electronic or athletic shoe to a child without teaching the worth of a dollar? In giving the child so much so soon, they have lost the awareness for sacrifice, and therefore, many have become entitled. I am in total agreement with creating a better environment and world for your child than the one in which you grew up. However, at what cost do we make these sacrifices?

I grew up in an era where you often heard, "A child should be seen and not heard." I abhorred that statement because I believe every child has a right to make their contribution in a respectful manner. Subsequently, the issue at hand is that a parent might feel manipulated or guilty into providing an item deemed excessive. In various instances, it is not a need but a want by the child. I agree this generation must deal with more issues than any other group ever had to handle. Bullying, peer pressure, drugs, abuse (physical, verbal, sexual, and emotional), traumatic violence, and mental illness to list a few of these issues. They have more knowledge and technology at their beck and call, yet It appears they are sadly lacking in necessary life skills. I surmise that, as adults, we have failed them.

In my homeland, most educational institutions are aligned with a denomination. We had daily devotions led by students and or the school chaplain. When I migrated to the United States, I was aghast by the notion that not all schools wore a uniform, much less God not being in schools. Having no God in schools is baffling. Have we as adults buried too much in our own self-interest to provide the attention that is needed for the children?

Do you believe that the electronic devices can do a better job at raising them? I was once told a story about a parent who was having her child sent for mental health services. She brought every electronic device for the child that was being admitted. When told that the child could not have these devices, the parent became angry. The parent in question was not able to understand how the staff was going to get a reasonable response from her child. She believed that giving the child the devices was the only way to keep the child occupied and engaged. This is not necessarily every parent's approach, but this scenario has become more prevalent in recent times. The story of Hannah reflects a parent who displayed a level of diligence, which is waning in today's society. Hannah was a conscientious parent and guarded the steps of her son's life with prayer.

Diligent Hannah

Hannah was the mother of Samuel, who was considered the greatest judge of his time. The idea of being a mother was initially foreign to her as she was unable to have a child and was teased by her rival, Penninah. This form of bullying wreaked havoc on her self-esteem. In today's society, she would have been presented with various methods to conceive a child. During Hannah's time, the only avenue open to her was prayer to God. The prayer which Hannah verbalized exuded the hallmark of a diligent parent. She prayed before the birth of her child and made a promise to dedicate the child's life to the Lord. The burden and anguish in her childless state was relieved when God answered her prayers and blessed her with a male child. She responded with praises of thanksgiving and continuous prayers throughout the life of her son Samuel.

Are the responsibilities of raising our children being relegated to technology?

In our focus to attain material items, are we helping or harming the child's development?

What type of legacy are you leaving for your children?

*****

Food for Thought: We need to realize that our children are a loan to us. The lessons we impart will keep them firmly planted or easily uprooted. God knew them (the children) before we met them, and we should follow His instructions. Are you helping or harming a child? The story of Hannah is a prime example of a diligent parent as she was prayerful prior to and after the birth of Samuel. Her story is told in 1 Samuel chapters 1 and 2. As goes the child, so goes society. "Lo, Children are a heritage of the Lord: and the fruit of the womb is his reward" (Psalm 127:3).

Word Power

Jamaican Proverb: "Kibba yuh mouth man."
Translation: Close your mouth.
Explanation: Control what you are saying or remain quiet.

"I hate you!"

"I quit!"

"I wish we were not related!"

"God, if you help me get this job the first paycheck is yours."

We are often guilty of words said in the heat of the moment or an impulsive promise made to God. Broken promises have all visited our doors in one fashion or another. Words said in anger or without thought have the power to do irreparable damage. There are many scriptures which speaks of rash decisions. One example is, "Be not rash with thy mouth, and let not thine heart be hasty to utter anything before God: for God is in heaven, and thou upon earth, therefore let thy words be few" (Ecclesiastes 5:2). Jephthah and the children who mocked Elisha paid a steep price for their words, and both cases caused pain and despair. It lays the cautionary tale to be mindful before you speak.

Jephthah's Rash Vow

> As Jephthah was preparing to go into battle, he made a request of God. He proclaimed:
>
> And Jephthah vowed a vow unto the Lord, and said, if thou shalt without fail deliver the children of Ammon into mine hands. Then it shall be, that whatsoever cometh forth of the doors of my house to meet me when I return in peace from the children of Ammon, shall surely be the Lord's and I will offer it up for a burnt offering.
>
> (Judges 11:30-31)

Jephthah's name means "He opens" in Hebrew, and it was reflected in his attitude in keeping his proclamations. His word was his bond, even when he spoke in a hasty manner. Jephthah was successful in battle against the children of Ammon and returned home in an excited mood. Upon his return home, the first person to greet him was his daughter. In fact, she was his only child. Jephthah became most distressed and tore his clothing as he realized the rash vow he had made with God. He owned his words even though it cost him great pain.

It is not certain if his daughter was physically sacrificed or exiled to another town, hence denying him continuation of his blood line, but he honored his vow with God. He spoke in anguish: "Alas my daughter! Thou hast brought me very low, and thou art one of them that trouble me: For

I have opened my mouth unto the Lord, and I cannot go back" (Judges 11:35). How many times in your life have you made promises but left them unfulfilled because they did not work to your advantage? As children, we use to say, "Sticks and stones may break my bones, but words cannot harm me." How far from the truth that was because, once words are released into the atmosphere, they do irreparable damage more so than physical harm. The children who teased Elisha paid with their lives and learned a deadly lesson.

Elisha Being Mocked by Children

Elisha was a mighty man of God. He replaced the prophet Elijah in bringing the Word to God's people. Unlike his predecessor Elijah, who was impassioned by nature, Elisha demonstrated God's power in a calm manner for all who sought God's grace. As a youngster, I would always say Elisha was anointed to the bones which Scripture proved to be true. That story is told in 2 Kings 13:21. Elisha displayed a compassionate heart when delivering God's message. However, whenever the name of God or His ministry was challenged, as was the case in the story of him being mocked, he demonstrated God's amazing power. Elisha was on his way from Bethel, and as he walked through the city he was met by a group of children. It may be surmised that as a prank they decided it would be fun to mock and tease Elisha:

> And he went up from thence unto Bethel: and as he was going up by the way, there came forth little children out of the city, and mocked him, and said unto him, go up, thou bald head; go up, thou bald

> head. And he turned back, and looked on them, and cursed them in the name of the Lord. And there came forth two she bears out of the wood, and tare forty and two children of them.
>
> 2 Kings 2:23-24

The cost of being killed is a serious consequence to pay for calling someone "Bald Head." I suspected, when the children awoke that morning, they did not believe that a "little teasing" would end their lives. They were simple words, which appeared to be harmless, but they had a devastating effect because of the way they were used. In both cases, lives were destroyed and sorrow was present. Words are potent, and, more importantly, they must be uttered with respect. My mom always said, "If you have nothing good to say, remain quiet." This is a true statement as there is life and death in words spoken.

*****

Food for Thought: Be aware of the words we place into the atmosphere as they can be costly. We should learn to formulate our words with wisdom and compassion. Avoid making promises to God when you are angry and impetuous. Our emotions should not dictate our speech. "The tongue has the power of life and death and those who love it will eat its fruit" (Proverbs 18:21 NIV).

Heart of Man

By Mindy Tucker

What if you could see the heart of man?
See the crime before it's done
Sense the plea for help from a troubled soul
Save the bounty from the robbers hold
What if you could see the heart of man?
View the love in his heart before the ring is won
Glimpse the pride and innocence of
a child for a chore well done
What if you could see the heart of man?
The motive behind a smile or lending a hand
What if you could see the heart of man?
A mother's love for her child or one abandoned
What if you could see the heart of man?
The heart of the homeless, the preacher,
the con man or the dapper one
Would you see patience, need, greed, or corruption?
What if you could see the heart of man?
Would outward appearance hide our
eyes from what's wrong?
What if you could see the heart of man?
Would religion, race, sex still stand on a pedestal?
Tell me really, what would you do if
you could see the heart of man?

Case of Mistaken Identity

Jamaican Proverb: "Yuh shake man hand yuh nuh shake him heart."

Translation: You shake a man's hand, you do not shake his heart.

Explanation: Do not make assumptions when dealing with others.

The truth will always come to light as nothing stays hidden forever. As my elders would say, "What happens in the night must come to light." We present beautiful outward facades but suffer inwardly. We deceive others with our appearances; we dye our hair to hide the fact it's greying. Waist-length hair is grown overnight. We buy fancy antiques, but the credit cards are maxed out. We drive cars which are beyond our budgets. A friend who worked in the financial sector once told me of an acquaintance who drove a Lexus van and had only the minimum balance in her account. The lady would often tell my friend she has a status to uphold. Society sees the Lexus and assumes wealth, but that lady is in a struggle to survive. Likewise, there are other areas where we misconstrue situations. Jacob deceived his father, Isaac. My friend Karen and I were almost placed in juvenile detention because our appearance did not reflect our ages.

The Truant Officer

Karen and I met when I migrated to the United States, we became fast friends. We complemented each other as we shared similar value systems. The fact that she possessed a sense of humor was a plus. Although we had similar personalities, we were completely different in behavioral components. I was fire, she was water. Karen was always calm in our discussions while I became deeply passionate. Many times, she had to soften my arguments because of my "brutal honesty." We often went shopping or discovered new places together. Karen and I were freshman and sophomore respectively at a college in New Jersey. Our appearances did not reflect that of the typical college students. In fact, we looked like high school students.

We realized that we had not seen our pre-college counselor in sometime and decided we needed to pay her a visit. On this day, our classes ended early. Karen and I boarded a bus that was headed towards the city of Newark. We were busy talking with each other, reflecting on our classes. As we looked out the window and recognized places that we thought looked familiar, we decided to get off at the next bus stop. Once off the bus, we were again lost in conversation and laughing up a storm.

There was a change in the environment, and our laughs were silenced. We noticed dilapidated buildings that were filled with graffiti, chipping paint, boarded up windows, or had bullet holes. We also observed discarded needles on the street and empty plastic baggies. Karen and I were lost and out of our element. The streets were deserted, and we were scared. I recall, as a child when asking for directions the residents of the town would say "Just around the corner." That around the corner direction would take you forever to get there. Now, Karen and I would love to see someone to ask for directions. We would be willing to walk miles if we could get to a familiar spot.

We quickened our pace as we attempted to find familiar landmarks. Karen and I were unable to find anything which appeared familiar. We were distressed as this was a time before Google Maps. Cellular telephones were just becoming common, and therefore not popular. We started mumbling words of a prayer. As we hurried towards the end of the street, we saw a yellow school bus which stopped in front of us. It was filled with children, their faces pressed against the windows. They were noisy, laughing, and pointing at us.

Karen and I were confused and wondered why the bus would be stopping in front of us. A tall, heavy set male stepped off the bus with a baseball bat in hand and said, "What high school y'all go to?" Now, we thought the man was joking. I laughed and Karen said in a tone of astonishment "High school? We are in college." The gentleman advanced towards us with a stern look on his face. About this time, the children on the bus started yelling, "Pick them up! Pick them up!" We looked at the face of the man and realized this was not a joke.

We started wondering how we were going to explain to our fathers that we were taken to a Juvenile Detention Center. Our fathers worked in different areas of the state and were vital members of their work force. Our brains were in overdrive as we processed our dilemma. How were we going to get out of this situation? We both had no answer to the question.

The man then said, "Y'all have any identification on you?" I reached into the back pocket of my jeans pants and handed him my college identification. Karen, however had forgotten her credentials, so I vouched for her. The man looked at us, shook his head and stepped back on the bus, all while the children were yelling, "Get on the bus! Pick them up!" We were mortified, but we were saved by a laminated piece of paper. Karen and I were judged by our appearance, and because of that, we were nearly locked up in the Juvenile Detention Center. The saying "Appearances can be deceiving" is proven true in the story of Isaac, Jacob, Esau, and Rebekah.

Isaac, Jacob, Esau, Rebekah, and the Stolen Blessing (*Genesis 27*)

Identity theft is a major crime in today's world. Jacob can be counted as one of the earliest perpetrators of this offense. He robbed his twin brother Esau of his blessing by deceiving their father Isaac. Esau was the older brother, loved by his father, was born with hairy skin, and loved the fields. Jacob was loved by his mother and believed in accumulating wealth for his own use. His father Isaac was old, and his eyesight was failing. Rebekah had favored one son over the other and was willing to deceive her husband. Isaac requested soup of Esau that he may bless him before he died. However, Esau was away in the fields, and his mother Rebekah heard the promise to bless him and plotted with her youngest son to deceive Isaac.

The Ruse

Rebekah assisted Jacob by making the soup and placing hairy animal skin on his arm to replicate Esau's skin. Jacob wore Esau's clothing which smelled of the field. After he had changed his appearance to look and feel like Esau, he went to his father to receive the blessing which was meant for his older brother. Isaac ate the food which Jacob presented, and then asked him to come close so that he could inspect him. "The voice is the voice of Jacob's, but the hands are the hands of Esau" (Genesis 27:22 NIV). Jacob realized that his voice would reveal his deception, and he attempted to alter his voice to sound like his brother's. Isaac ate, drank, and embraced his son and smelled his clothing. All the while thinking he was blessing Esau; the deception was completed. He blessed the wrong son. Jacob was comfortable after he had achieved his stated goal of material gain.

Rebekah and Jacob conspired after the identity theft was completed. When Esau returned from the field after a hard day at work, he realized the deceptive act his brother and mother had committed. He was furious and threatened to kill his brother because of his duplicity. Rebekah further encouraged the deception by encouraging Jacob to run to his uncle Laban, who lived far away. There was a lot of loss in that one act of deception. Isaac went to his grave knowing he blessed the wrong child. Esau's relationship with Jacob was damaged and would take years to be repaired. Rebekah chose sides between her children and participated in the deception. In essence, she lost both her sons because of trickery.

How often have you misjudged a situation based on appearance?

Are you guilty of hiding behind the proverbial mask?

Are there instances where you have missed a blessing because you made a judgement call on someone's appearance?

*****

Food for Thought: We change our appearances daily for various reasons. In certain cases, that change can be viewed as deceptive. God never looks at the outward appearance, he looks at the heart of man. "Look not at his countenance or on the height of his stature, because I have refused him for the Lord seeth not as man seeth; for man looketh at the outward appearance, but the Lord looketh on the heart" (1 Samuel 16:7).

Unwelcome Spirits

"In the beginning was the Word, and the Word was with God and the Word was God."

John 1:1

Growing up in my homeland, I often heard the term "Obeah." It is a form of walking on the dark side, although the purveyors of the practice will say otherwise. This belief of Obeah is subsumed in minuscule parts of the culture. I remember once in my high school physical education class we were being taught the basics of volleyball. Our teacher was instructing us on the correct manner in which to serve the ball. Our playing field was suspected to be located next door to the balm yard for the "Spiritual Leader," Mother R. My classmates and I had heard many stories over the years about her mystical practice and Obeah.

My fellow student got ready to serve the ball. She hit the ball with such power that, instead of the ball going over the net, it went over the fence and into the yard of Mother R. Silence fell on the court. We were surprised when the ball was thrown back over the wall. Nobody went to pick the ball up as some of us believed it was cursed. There were some of us that kept our distance from the ball while others just shrugged and said it was stupid.

Entrance Ways

Fast forward years later to the clamor of *Harry Potter* and the *Twilight* series. This compilation of written words has made millions of dollars in theater and book sales. Make no mistake about the reception it has garnered in society. These written works are not being called stupid. The contents of these books are devoured with excited fervor and bated breath. *Yet how many of you have read the Bible in a similar manner?* As individuals, we innocently watch and read these materials, unknowingly opening our spirits to unimaginable intrusions.

Years ago, in graduate school, I was juggling many responsibilities. I had an internship, worked part time, had responsibilities at church, and carried a full-time academic course load. One might say I was overwhelmed, and it reflected in my outward appearance. My favorite words to say at that time were, "I am tired." I often wished I could press a button and get every task accomplished. One day, as I sat in the park in front of one of my internship's sites, a lady approached me. She appeared to be harmless, and she began a conversation. She spoke about the weather and other innocuous topics. I was vague but polite in my responses to her. The next words out of her mouth came out of left field. She said, "I sense a lot of pain. Let me see your palms. I can read your future." I thought, *Is she for real?*

The intrigue to let her go ahead and read my palm was powerfully tempting. As I contemplated what next to do, a thought popped into my head, "Darkness disguised as Light." I smiled at her and told her no, but she insisted. I politely excused myself from her company, thanks to the to the still small voice—my conscience. God is the only one who knows the future. Let us not get caught up in the net of intrigue. After this encounter, I wondered the following:

> *How many individuals have invested in horoscopes, tarot cards, and mediums, hoping for future answers?*
>
> *Are you opening doorways which seemingly are not harmful?*
>
> *How often have you ignored that still small voice?*
>
> *As individuals, we should stop believing in the stars and the person who reads the stars and begin believing instead in the God, who created them.*

The Souvenir Shop

I love traveling. There is an abundant amount of information to be learned from other cultures. I try to do as much research about my destination as I possibly can. Whenever I plan my trips, I endeavor to incorporate good food, fascinating history, beautiful scenery, and lots of walking. My travel friends will attest to all four. A few years ago, we traveled to the "Pearl of Aegean," or Izmir, Turkey. It was a beguiling visit.

We were a group of five girls out to explore an old city. It was quiet and peaceful when we disembarked our cruise ship and started walking towards the town. There were dogs sitting out in the sun near the sidewalk cafés. The seafront was calm and beautiful. It was packed with personal boats and passenger ferries. One of my friends, minutes into our walk, stated she was returning to the ship with no explanations given. We thought it strange that she would return, but we kept walking. The search was on for souvenir shops. I was admiring the history of the old city.

I was wondering, *Who had walked these streets years before me?*

If I were transported back in time, what part would I play in this society?

As time came close for us to return, we found a souvenir shop. We all walked into the shop. I was the last person to enter, and an uncomfortable feeling came over me. The hairs on the back of my neck stood up, and my spirit became incredibly angry. I ignored the feeling, and we started buying souvenirs. I could not continue to ignore my reaction, and, before I exited the store, I placed the items I had picked up back on the shelves. I told my friends "Don't buy anything else, and whatever you have bought, we are going to throw it away." I thought I had lost my mind in saying this to them. My friends were supportive. I kept thinking: we came this far, and I was telling them to discard the items purchased?

I was not able to shake the irate feeling. The storekeeper was disappointed and tried to show us other crafts in the store. The items were well constructed and displayed a high level of craftsmanship. As we got back to the ship, my friend that had initially returned explained that she had a bad feeling. She said that the hairs were standing on the back of her neck as soon as she had disembarked the ship. I looked at her in utter shock as there was no way she could have known I shared a similar experience.

The Witch of Endor and Saul

Saul was an anointed king by God. In fact, he was the first king of Israel. He had his faults, but God chose him. Samuel, who anointed him king, was dead, and he needed to seek counsel. He was not getting responses to his prayers or answers from the prophets. Saul had lost his way and was no longer in favor with God. One might say he had a tormented spirit. I suspected Saul became impatient and frustrated with the lack of answers. How many times have you fallen into that trap? Where you become tempted to call the psychic hotline, have your palms, or tarot cards read? All are seemingly innocent activities, but are we giving permission for diabolic forces to enter our lives?

Saul forgot about God's prior goodness in his consultation with the Witch of Endor: "Then said Saul unto servants, seek me a woman that hath a familiar spirit, that I may go to her, and enquire of her. And his servants said to him, Behold, there is a woman that hath a familiar spirit at Endor" (1 Samuel 28:7). King Saul was able to visit with the witch but was distraught at the message which he received. The king decided to take matters into his own hands. He disguised himself and approached the witch, asking her to bring forth Samuel. Once the Witch of Endor realized that this was King Saul, she feared for her life because she realized his deceit. The witch was able to make contact to the spirit world, and Samuel did come forth. The conversation was as follows:

> And Samuel said unto Saul, Why has thou disquieted me, to bring me up? And Saul answered, I am sore distressed; for the Philistines make war against me, and God is departed from me, and answereth

> me no more, neither by prophets, nor by dreams: therefore, I have called thee, that thou mayest make known unto me what I shall do. Then said Samuel, Wherefore then dost thou ask of me, seeing the Lord is departed from thee, and is become thine enemy?
>
> 1 Samuel 28:15-16

Saul was sore displeased when Samuel confirmed what he had suspected that the Lord was gone from him. However, his temperament became sullener as Samuel continued to speak. "Because thou obeyest not the voice of the Lord, nor executedst his fierce wrath upon Amalek, therefore the Lord had done this thing unto thee this day. Moreover, the Lord will also deliver Israel with thee into the hands of the Philistines: and tomorrow shalt thou and thy sons be with me: The Lord also shall deliver the host of Israel into the hand of the Philistines" (1 Samuel 28:18-19).

Saul, who was once an anointed man of God, would face dire consequences because he had strayed from the path which God had set before him. Let us not fall prey to our emotions and turn to outlets other than God for guidance about our life. The power of God is not to be trifled with. It is not for our whims and fancy.

*****

Food for Thought: Beware that not everything that is appealing to the eyes should be carried into our homes. Display vigilance always with whom or what you give access to the doorways of your lives. Finding avenues outside of God for peace and clarity is not the answer.

Shockwaves

By Mindy Tucker

Never seen anything like this in all my days
I have to break my neck to see the top of the place
Noise all around me I feel like am in a rat race
Better yet it feels like shockwaves
What you mean you have more than your ears pierced?
What is up with your hair it makes the rainbow look tame?
Eastside of the city or the Westside?
I don't care just give me directions
Is my destination near?
Why are they wasting the eggs?
When so much hunger abounds
What in the world is Halloween?
Thanksgiving for life I give everyday
But you celebrate with a turkey on this day, shockwaves
Change in climate is messing up my skin
Three layers of clothing this is maddening
Your spelling is messed up but you correct mine
I need to deposit a cheque in the bank and check the time
When you say check, both spell the same
Am in a state of confusion, Shockwaves
That was years ago
I have grown to appreciate and adjust to the nuances
Once novelty now seems normal
The Good Shepherd is my anchor in the midst of the storm
Shockwaves, No Problem
Just cultures saying hello

Stranger in a Strange Land

"How shall we sing the Lord's song in a strange land?"
Psalm 137:4

I arrived in the United States of America in the fall season. I was in awe of the changing foliage in multiple colors. The move presented a variety of prospects, interesting histories, awesome experiences, and challenges. These encounters made the transition mystifying at times. To say I had culture shock would be an understatement. There were instances where being female, immigrant, and black were highlighted. Often, I was reminded that I would have to be twice as good as my white counterparts. I had to deal with many changes: "weird" holidays, living with my dad for the first time in years, racism, the fast-paced society, and changing seasons these were just some of the deviations.

I grappled with the fact the many schools did not require a uniform to be worn. Consequently, when I did enter the school system, I watched as teachers circled the words *colour* and *cheque* which here was spelt color and check. The word color, I could understand, but there was no way to immediately differentiate between the word 'check' unless they were used in a sentence. My teachers and I had many discussions about spelling.

Football in the United States is called soccer. Where I am from and in most other countries, it is just football. Primarily, the version of football I am familiar with it is played with the feet. The American version of football is played primarily with the hands. It reminded me of the game, rugby. Nothing made sense to me anymore. I figured this was how the Hebrew boys Daniel, Shadrack, Meshach, and Abednego felt when they were captured and brought to Babylon.

Color of Skin Versus Class

I never utterly understood the entire scope of racism. The land of my birth is primarily known for jerk chicken, beautiful beaches, reggae music, and world class sprinters. However, it has a class system or classism and, to a lesser extent, colorism. One may infer this was spewed from the bowels of British colonialism. I recalled in high school, whenever my classmates would graduate, often they would not be able to obtain a job. I was baffled by this occurrence until I was able to speak with one of my teachers. She was able to explain the root cause of the rejections at the time. It appeared that some of their applications were being denied because they listed inner-city addresses. How could they judge my friends and acquaintances without giving them a chance? I smiled to myself because, years earlier, I had made the same judgment call in relation to the location of my school.

I am of two opinions in relation to race:

1. Your race was predestined, thereby giving you no choice.
2. You may change your address but not the color of your skin.

Although, over the years, many have tried to alter their skin tone by using certain chemicals, to the detriment of their health, but I digress. In Jamaica, the term "Browning" was used to represent individuals that were of a lighter complexion. The way the term was used would be viewed today as harassment. Many times, the expression was being heckled by males standing on the street corners. Utterings, such as "Browning" or "Baby Love," would be shouted as was the practice at that time. No perceived physical harm was done, but the receiver of the heckling often suffered in uncomfortable silence.

The disdain for the color of one's skin was taken to another level and plain to see in many of my interactions in my new home country. These exchanges, or palpable microaggressions, brought anxiety, confusion, and, at times, fear of harm. I recall, each time I was in a store, there would be someone watching me from aisle to aisle. At first, I thought, "That's nice. They are there to help." However, as it became more pronounced and frequent, I realized I was being watched.

I became accustomed to seeing white ladies clutch their purses when I would pass by. However, this reaction depended upon the neighborhood. Racism occurred in other forms, some subtle and others ignorant. There were other cases where the questions and actions of a few of my white classmates and other individuals made me shudder. They would comment on my diction and asked how well-spoken I was, or say, "Is that all your hair? It is so long" and "It is soft." At times, they would touch my hair without permission and ask about my hair care. This made me uncomfortable, like an exhibit on show if you will. I was confused as to their obsession with my hair. What does it matter the length or texture? I did not see them asking any of the Caucasian classmates or others about their hair. There were many days where I felt like asking:

"Why are you always dressed in black?"

"Why do you have a tattoo?"

"Why do you have body piercings?"

"Why is your hair purple?"

But I learned to choose my battles carefully.

Trick or Treat

Outside of racism, one of the hardest celebrated traditions to be understood upon migrating was Halloween. I called it the "weird" or "dark" holiday. I believed it was supporting evil and living in a world of make-belief. Children were observed throwing eggs at cars and buses. They tossed toilet paper on people's homes. I thought to myself, *This place is nuts!* Such waste. Many people were dying of hunger, and they were wasting eggs. The children dressed up in costumes and asked for candy. I did not comprehend this; you were being given lots of candy at the detriment of your teeth. My family is a staunch proponent for teeth health. *These parents were irresponsible*, was my thought.

Ability to Adapt

During this time period, based on my dad's behavior, it felt as if I was still that four-year-old child sitting in the back of the taxicab instead of a teenager. Our relationship was being rebuilt, and we were getting reacquainted with each other. We often had our disagreements. I love Dad, and I surmised his responses were from a place of concern—but it felt stifling. I felt isolated as my current social circle did not reflect my fun-loving personality.

I now dressed in layers of clothing, I learned how to walk on ice, and after injuring my fingertips from the cold, I realized the necessity for gloves. My first snowfall was a thing of beauty. However, in the days that followed, it started to melt and the beauty was replaced with slush and mud. Years later, I would reflect on the first experience of snowfall and its aftermath, and how life often resembles beauty but presents disappointments.

Teachers were circling my spelling, and I felt I was not smart enough. This was a bruise to my ego and self-confidence. I came from an educational system where, at the time, children began high school between the average ages of ten to twelve years old. Our curriculum exposed us to many topics at an early age. Now teachers were circling my work! If I learned anything from this experience, it taught me humility.

Would I ever be able to adjust to all these changes? However, there was one constant stabilizer in the form of the church. My dad was a member of an established church, and I was eventually able to meet new friends. It gave me a sense of comfort and stability. If I felt like this in my adjustment period, I could only imagine the Hebrew boys in Babylon, and I was not being held captive.

The Hebrew Boys in a Pagan Land

Hananiah (Shadrach), Mishael (Meshach), Azariah (Abednego), and Daniel (Belteshazzar) were all taken from their homeland of Jerusalem and held as captives in Babylon. The land of Babylon was rife with idolatry, debauchery, and lawlessness which ran contrary to their principles. When they became captives, they lost their names, which were especially important in their culture. In doing so, they lost a piece of their identity and their way of living. However, they found favor with the leader of the Eunuchs, who was placed in charge of them. They were given into the service of King Nebuchadnezzar because they were among the brightest and best of the captives.

Daniel and his friends were staunch believers in God and wrestled with the new way of life in this land. The style of the Babylonian eating was different as well as their ways of worship. The foods in the new land were considered rich, and Daniel pledged not to defile himself. In Babylon, they worshipped many gods, while Daniel and his friends worshipped one God. They decided that they would prove to the king that their way of eating was healthier, and Daniel spoke with the eunuch placed in charge of them. "Prove thy servants, I beseech thee, ten days; and let them give us pulse (fruits and vegetables) to eat and water to drink. Then let our countenances be looked upon before thee, and the countenances of the children that eat of the portion of the king's meat: and as thou seest; deal with thy servants." (Daniel 1:12-13).

The request which was made by Daniel was met, and after ten days, the Hebrew boys looked healthier than the children that ate the king's food. They faced other obstacles in this foreign land: Shadrach, Meshach, and Abednego were thrown in the burning furnace because they did not bow to the golden image. However, God delivered them from the fiery furnace by standing with them. Nebuchadnezzar placed three men in the fire but observed four. He was convinced of the awesome power of the Hebrew boys' God after witnessing this divine intervention. Daniel was thrown in the Lion's Den because he was praying to God. He was delivered from the Lion's Den as God closed the mouths of the lions. In each challenge, they faced that God was in the midst, and He took care of them. God was the only constant figure in their lives. He is ever faithful and unchanging.

Have you sacrificed a value to belong in a group or setting?

*****

Food for Thought: We can adjust to changes without altering our convictions or belief systems. God is never-changing, and He will be there for you in the face of adversity. "The grass withereth, the flower fadeth, but the word of God will stand forever" (Isaiah 40:8).

Suffer the Little Children

"And who so shall receive one such little
child in my name receiveth me."
Matthew 18:5

I love working and playing with children. I think they are game changers, smart, funny, resilient, and observant. Growing up, I was surrounded by a loving family, but I always wanted the attention of my older siblings. I was the youngest and the typical "annoying little sister." I wanted to emulate my siblings. I would try to listen to conversations my siblings were having. When they realized I was trying to listen to their communication, they spoke in "Gypsy," a type of secret code similar to Pig Latin. I learned to speak in "Gypsy." They started spelling their words. I learned to spell. Then they began closing the bedroom door. I would then use a drinking glass to press to the outside of the door to listen. At times, I got the impression that I was a bother to them. Everything they did, I reported to Mom, and they called me "The Chatterbox."

Occasionally, my siblings would include me in an activity. They taught me to play the board games Scrabble and Ludo. I never won at either game, but I was included. There were days when my brother and his friends would "run a boat." That is, cook a meal which usually consisted of at least two pounds of rice or "flour" (dumplings) and three to four pounds of curried chicken back with some "wash," which would be equivalent to a glass of lemonade. When we did not have a cooked meal, we enjoyed spiced bun with cheese and a glass of milk. Although their inclusion made me feel welcomed, there were other times when I was reminded I was a child.

Bus Runnings

The Jolly bus or Jamaica Omni Bus (J.O.S.) was the government bus system which would later be replaced by private minibuses. These buses had names such as "Exterminator," "Morning Ride," "Indian Sun," "Suzette," and "Shaka Zulu." They had no set bus schedule—just a route. Also, there were the illegal buses, which were called "robots," that capitalized on the disorganization of the system. However, whether it was a robot or a legal minibus, they both had one thing in common: they did not want to fill their buses with school children or "schoolers" as we were condescendingly called by the conductors. The "schoolers" were treated with little or no regard. The rationale was that they only wanted adults as the fares of the "schoolers" could not give much of a profit for the vehicle.

If the conductors were desperate, they would allow the students on the buses. However, as soon as an adult entered the bus, we had to relinquish our seats. Many times, they would say to the schoolers, "Small up yuhself." In this instance, we would be required to give the adults room to be seated in the bus. This caused problems at times as not all of us schoolers were compliant. There were those who believed that their 50 or 60 cents was just as good as the adult's $1.30. We were expected to wait outside in any weather until the seats on the buses were filled before we entered the bus. Many times, we were left behind at the bus stop and ended up being late for school. Early on in life, you got the message that you were not as valued as an adult. I took these lessons and vowed never to treat a child in this manner.

Summer Visit

One summer before I returned to school, some of my siblings were visiting. I was overly excited to see them. I tried not being a nuisance and was on my best behavior. They inquired about school and my friends. I gave them space and remained quiet when not in the conversation. One day, they made plans to visit Ocho Rios, a popular tourist town. I got overly excited because we were going for a ride in the country. However, I noticed I was not included in their plans. There was no preparation being made to assist in getting me dressed.

I was very hurt and went to the bathroom to cry. One sister inquired if I was coming and was told no with what appeared to be valid reasoning at that time. It was assumed I would take a long period to get dressed. My sister found me in the bathroom and washed my feet as I cried. I was not invited to go with my family members that day. I was left home alone. As the younger sibling, I guess I would appear to be an annoyance. However, the kind action of my sister spoke volumes to my heart. Children are to be loved and cared for.

Jesus Blessed the Children

As Jesus sat one day with the disciples, children were brought to him to blessed. His disciples became angry and rebuked the children. Jesus explained to the disciples that they should not stop the children from coming to see him. Jesus lovingly said, "Suffer the little children, and forbid them not, to come unto me for such is the Kingdom of heaven" (Matthew 19:14). Children are special to Jesus, and they should be treated with respect and understanding.

A child is innocent and looks at the world with trusting eyes. It is our job to nurture that trust as the seeds we plant today affect the next generation. Children are such prized possessions to God that, if you harm a child or alter their belief system, there will be severe punishment for the offending party. Jesus warned, "It were better for him that a millstone was hanged about his neck and he cast into the sea, than that he should offend one of these little ones" (Luke 17:2). Children should be supported by a loving family unit, but that is not always the case. Many are abused, kidnapped, trafficked, left homeless for various reasons, or killed.

Are you condoning the mistreatment of a child out of fear?

Do you limit your time with children because you find them annoying?

*****

Food for Thought: We need to display childlike faith in our belief system. It is our job to care for children, not harm them. Most importantly, the channels of communication should be kept open with our children—not only should we hear them, we should listen. Invest in a child, and the deposits you make today may be your saving grace tomorrow.

Jealous God

"Thou shalt have no other gods before me."
Exodus 20:3

Jesus Christ is the living God!

The Apostle John made a similar proclamation: "In the beginning was the Word, and the Word was with God and the Word was God" (John 1:1). He is a jealous God, but He is also just and fair. God has given us free will. It is that will that permeates our lives with choices. However, we have occupied our minds and time with many options. As a society, we have become tethered to many gods. Some of which are video games, the internet, the shopping mall, social media, fame, fortune, our outward appearance, and our jobs.

Temporary Gods

Many have achieved the highest awards in their chosen professions. These accolades consist of various materials which will fade, rust, and collect dust over time, yet they are highly cherished. In many respects, one may infer they have become our gods. However, the gospel of Mark 8:36 speaks of gaining worldly fame and possessions yet losing the only thing that matters to God, our soul. Consequently, highlighting the fact that anything which consumes most of our lives, leaving us no time in God's presence, is a god. Our created gods are temporary, fleeting, and have no life.

There are many religions today, and each one has their representative of a higher being. Several individuals are of the opinion that there are many different paths to God. When traveling, I enjoy learning about the local cultures outside of the outlined travel schedule. Often, I would observe many different styles of worship and how they choose to pay respect to their gods. My place is not to judge or question a person's choice; it is to display qualities which reflect Christ. As we have free will, and all will come to an understanding that Jesus is Lord. Scripture states, "And that every tongue should confess that Jesus Christ is Lord, to the glory of God the Father" (Philippians 2:11).

Several of the popular gods in biblical days were Baal, Dagon, and Marduk, and they were revered. The inhabitants of these lands offered gifts, sacrifices, and worshipped these idols. However, all were fleeting and eventually destroyed. We cannot force people to serve God. Mankind must experience a softening or conviction of the heart of their own free will. The Bible says that Jesus is the only way to God. "I am the way, and the truth, and the life. No man cometh unto the Father but by me" (John 14:6).

Jamaica is a mainly Christian nation and, at some point in history, had more churches per square mile than any other country in the world. The irony is that they also had just as many bars. The wit of my culture, the rum bar, and the church. I grew up in this environment, and God was my only way. However, once I migrated, the differences in belief systems, and in some cases the lack of a belief system, became prominent. It was a delicate balance of understanding. This understanding would enable me to carefully traverse other cultures.

Land of Lakes and Volcanoes

Nicaragua reminded me of the land of my birth with its lush vegetation and variety of fruits, especially the guineps. I enjoyed the crack of the tangy fruit, slippery in texture and slightly sour in taste as I crunched the seed. The little girls with ribbons in their hair reminded me of simpler times. The green land scape and tropical flowers brought back pleasant memories. I ate some of the best beef in recent memory. I later learned that it was farm-raised beef.

There was another side which drew my interest in the vast history of this land. It had a mixed history of political wars and violence but also a kind, resilient, and creative people. It boasted one of the oldest church's in the Americas: Our Lady of the Assumption Cathedral in Granada. Originally built in the 1500s, the structure still stands today and has been refurbished over the years. Craft markets displayed talent unparalleled. I was enthralled with the power and beauty of an active volcano. My sister and I had the pleasure of visiting one such volcano.

Awesome Volcanic Power

I looked at the vast expanse of power, beauty, and danger in front of me and thought, *What an awesome God!* This active volcano truly displayed God's power. Our tour guide gave us instructions to avoid the edge and, if the horn was blown, to move swiftly from the edge. The gases and the heat being emitted were dangerous and gave off a noxious smell. I thought it was beauty and danger all in one package. The tour guide gave us brief facts about the volcano and the history of the location. There was one moment in his summary that made me cringe. Whenever, the gods were angry, female virgins were drugged and would be thrown alive in the interior of the volcano to soothe the anger of the gods. Whether this is fact or not, I have no proof, but it was thought provoking.

One member of my tour group was not happy with the information from the tour guide. She said, "Why could it not be male virgins? The poor woman always suffers." Unlike her, my mind went in another direction. Alleged human sacrifice to the gods. I could not parlay this with my upbringing. I know of only one God, but earlier societies appeased many gods. This was the only way of life the natives allegedly knew. Likewise, Christianity was all I knew. Unlike the Israelites, who were exposed to God and saw his daily miraculous splendor, and yet they chose to the worship The Golden Calf idol.

The Worship of the Golden Calf *(Exodus 32:1-24)*

After being delivered out of the land of Egypt, the children of Israel were growing restless. Moses had been delayed on Mount Sinai as he was receiving The Ten Commandments from God. The people appealed to Aaron for his guidance in Moses' absence as they had become bored. Aaron who was Moses' brother had a pliable personality and asked that all the gold jewelry be brought to him. They created a Golden Calf similar to the ones which were worshipped in the land of Egypt. There was singing and dancing, thinking they were being sincere in their worship, but they were being disobedient to God's command. They were ignoring the command which the Lord had given to worship no graven image. A marvelous time was being had by all parties involved.

God was ready to destroy the children of Israel when he witnessed their behavior of idol worshipping. However, Moses pleaded for mercy on their behalf; God acquiesced and offered them another chance. He is a God of many chances. Upon his descent from Mount Sinai, Moses was livid at the behavior of the people. He destroyed the Golden Calf, and then made them drink the ash and water from its destruction. Moses interceded for the people with God, and in His infinite mercy and wisdom, He relented from destruction. As I reflected on this biblical story, I wondered on the following questions for the lives of mankind today:

How many present day idols do you have in your life?

What happens after you appease the gods in your life, whatever they may be?

*****

Food for Thought: "For I will be merciful to their unrighteousness and their sins and their inequities I will remember their sins no more" (Hebrews 8:12). God is forgiving, patient, and fair in all things. Christ shed his blood that we may live, and the ultimate thank you is to worship Him.

Essence of Life

By Mindy Tucker

Curious how life seems to pass you by
Funny how you live and then you die
The essence of their life is not one of beauty
But of pain, shame and survival
The invisible generation, they belong to no one nation
Yet they breath, eat and sleep not knowing
when will be there last beat
They represent many colors and creeds
Yet they are viewed as faceless, nameless and shameless
Society does not show a care
They scream for help from their very core
They are battered and bruised and often refused
They are homeless and their lifestyles may
not fit the picture of perfection
Yet they rise to face another day struggling to survive
Not knowing what fate, they will meet on the street
Here in lies the essence of their lives
Survivors
Yes, they are wise beyond their years their burdens are heavy
Still they breathe, eat and sleep
This is the essence of their lives
Talented
A word becomes a motion
Motion gives life to calm
Calm gives life a song
A song gives life to a story
A story opens a wound
Here in lies the essence of their lives

For Your Good

African Proverb: "The axe forgets, the tree remembers."
Explanation: The person who harms forgets, but he who is harmed remembers.

"A fi yuh own good." Growing up, these words were heard often by myself and many of my friends. I did not like hearing these words because they were usually connected to a medicine, herb, or being told you could not play with a friend. I loved playing with my friend Jasmine. She lived next door. At seven, we were the best of pals. We loved making mud pies or, in my Jamaican vernacular, "Dutty Pot," with gypsum dust, water, and dirt. Jasmine would climb the cherry tree and we would eat our fill of cherries and coconut cookies. We played school, restaurant, hairdresser, and created outfits for our dolls. Jasmine and I enjoyed a bounty of organic fruits before organic became mainstream: between our homes we had mangoes, watermelons, soursops, pomegranates, cherries, and papayas.

We communicated through the fence which separated our houses and at times played in each other's yard. We frolicked our days away. Many days, I would hear from my brother, "Time to take your book. It's for your own good." To our seven-year-old minds, my brother was being mean. Another time, you heard from my mom, "Drink it, it good fi yuh." On these occasions, when I was told to drink "wash out" or cleansing herbs, it usually signaled the end of the summer holidays. Everything was always for your good, but to the person on the receiving end, it appeared that it was meant to harm.

A Betrayal in Kind

In my second semester of graduate school, I heard some semblance of the words, "We have nothing in common anymore." These words were being uttered by someone I considered a friend. We were like a house on fire. Now, it seemed that the house was being burnt down. Frankly, I developed a heavily dependent bond, almost like a crutch. So, when the words were uttered, they cut to the core, and I was hurt. My friend appeared calm and concerned. I felt betrayed, given the experiences we shared together. There was a void when she left. I battled through feelings of anger and betrayal.

This betrayal made me cautious when meeting new people. However, I came to the realization that, regardless of the pain it caused, it was for my own good. I count it as a lesson well learned as it was truly a betrayal in kind. This was a major catalyst in propelling my growth and development. This progressing would not have happened had I not been emotionally hurt. There is goodness hidden in every hurt as witnessed by Joseph and his interactions with his brothers.

Coat of Many Colors

Jacob had many children, but he loved Joseph the best of all. He was enamored by Joseph as he was born in the latter stages of his life. To prove his love, Jacob made his beloved son a coat of many colors. Joseph loved his father, but he was boastful towards his brothers. He was a dreamer and would often boast to his brothers of these dreams. Joseph was often in a position of power in these dreams, and he would lord it over his brothers. They hated him because he had their father's love, he was arrogant, and he had the coat of many colors.

The brothers decided they would teach Joseph a lesson. They were working in the field, and he was asked to bring them lunch. His brothers saw him approaching, and they plotted to harm him because of their dislike for him. However, his brother Ruben interceded and asked that Joseph not be harmed but be thrown instead in a pit. The brothers agreed and threw Joseph in the pit and dipped his coat of many colors in the blood of an animal. The brothers told their father that Joseph was dead. Jacob was devastated to hear of the death of his favorite son. Unknowing to Jacob, the brothers had sold Joseph into slavery.

Once in the land of Egypt, his brothers' betrayal set Joseph's life on a path which would one day save their lives and their families. Joseph went from the pit, to being a slave in Potiphar's house, to being thrown in prison with false evidence, to prime minister providing for many nations. Joseph was able to forgive his brothers for their cruelty and treated them with kindness. His brothers meant to harm him, but the path laid before him was for his own good. Joseph stated to his brothers, "But as for you, Ye thought evil against me; but God meant it unto good to bring to pass, as it is this day, to save much people alive" (Genesis 50:20). His storied life worked out for his own good from the pit, to Potiphar's house, to prisoner, to prime minister. It can be said his destiny was deferred, not prevented.

*****

Food for Thought: Amid betrayals and hurts, the pain might appear never-ending, but good will come from that pain. Remember the ultimate betrayal was of Judas to Christ. It brought initial pain but provided eternal life for all who accepts Jesus Christ. You may also think of a caterpillar evolving from their cocoon to a butterfly. The process appears painful to break the casing, but the result is a beautiful butterfly. 1 Corinthians 7:35 (NIV) states, "I am saying this for your own good, not to restrict you, but that you may live in a right way in undivided devotion to the Lord."

Friendship is a Gem

"A friend loveth at all times, and a
brother is born for adversity."

Proverbs 17:17

Friend and acquaintance are two words which we often confuse in our daily lives. Growing up, most of my colleagues and I often heard the term "fair-weather friends" spoken by our elders. It was a warning to us to be able differentiate between a friend and an acquaintance. A friend is a person who sticks with someone through the good and the bad times. An acquaintance is someone who you have limited knowledge of. I enjoyed being with my friends; they were a dynamic set of girls. I will explore the friendship I shared with my mates. Also, review the love and loyalty in the friendship of David and Jonathan.

Friends

I had many acquaintances in high school but few friendships. Abigail, Debbie, and Rachel were my friends and shared many of my high school experiences. We were a collection of personalities and were often seen together. Abigail was smart, quiet, and loyal. Debbie was astute, had a dynamic sense of humor, and reliable. Rachel was keen, ambitious, and adept in the fashion department. Me, I was the enigma. I had a sense of humor, outgoing, witty, but shy. There were times when we were serious and reflective, but for the most part, we had fun. We shared many adventures together. They introduced me to sporting events and functions at the National Stadium and National Arena, respectively. I, in turn, took them on many hikes, and sometimes they would accompany me to my church functions, rehearsals, and performances. Abigail was usually the one who did the latter duties. However, I remember an incident where I questioned if I was being a good friend to Abigail.

The Jewelry Thief

One Sunday afternoon at the end of church, Abigail and I were walking home. We were busy chatting and laughing as we usually did when we were together. I noticed a suspicious looking young man trailing us in the distance. I made Abigail aware of his presence, and I began walking fast. Abigail's pace was slower as her skirt was longer and prevented easy movement. I was close to the bottom of the street before I realized that my friend was not with me. I turned to observe the thief stripping my friend of her jewelry at knifepoint. He ran off in the opposite direction from us. I felt anger towards the robber but concern for my friend. When Abigail caught up with me, I asked, out of a feeling of guilt, "Why didn't you walk faster?" She explained about the length of her skirt. We decided we needed to report the incident to the police.

The policemen were amazed that, since we were both walking together, my friend got robbed while I still had my jewelry. I remember the police saying, "You left your friend alone?" I felt like the lowest of the low. My teenage self had responded in fear. Could I have done more? I might never be able to adequately answer that question. However, this experience informed future vigilance of my surroundings and using wisdom in situations. I now look back at the situation and realized how blessed we were. The robbery could have ended differently. David shared an opposite experience with Jonathan where his loyalty was never in question.

David and Johnathan (*1 Samuel 18:1-4*)

Johnathan and David shared a bond which went deep to the soul. King Saul, Johnathan's father, became jealous of David as the women sang of David's prowess in battle. They noted that Saul had killed thousands but David ten thousand. Once he heard that someone had supplanted his military greatness, he was envious. In essence, he tried to kill David while under the influence of an evil spirit. However, David had the favor of God and was spared. The fact that David was spared scared Saul as he realized he was no longer in favor with God. Saul knew what it meant to have God's favor on his life.

A Covetous Streak

Saul continuously tried to kill David, and he fled to his friend Jonathan. 1 Samuel 20:1 says, "What have I done? What is mine iniquity? And what is my sin before thy father that he seeketh my life?" He was able to save David's life by arranging his escape. Saul was angry at his son Jonathan, for helping David, who he was jealous of. There are many ways in which Jonathan could have assisted his father, but he loved David. Instead, he asked David to promise to be kind to his bloodline. He was loyal and loving even though David angered his father King Saul. Jonathan displayed loyalty and love towards David beyond compare. As individuals, we should aspire to display these qualities to our friends.

*****

Food for Thought: A friend will always love you. Choose your friends wisely. As a child, the elders would always say, "Show me your friends and I will tell you who you are." Many times, this was reflective of the company one kept. Not everyone should be given permission to enter your friendship circle. "He that walketh with wise men shall be wise: but a companion of fools shall be destroyed" (Proverbs 13:20).

Potentially Talented

"Whatever you do, work at it with all your heart, as working for the Lord, not for human masters."
Colossians 3:23 NIV

My friend Peter and I were having a stirring conversation about someone's potential. He would always say, "There is a lot of duppy potential in the graveyard." Hearing him say that hit a sore spot. He made this statement as he was holding a collection of my unpublished poetry. He was also of a creative mind, and I respected his opinions. Was he directing that statement at me? His comment got me thinking. Other individuals have always seen more in me than I could see in myself. I was reminded of the parable of "The Ten Talents."

The Talents

The parable in the book of Mathew chapter 25:14-30 speaks of a master distributing talents to his workers. To each worker, he gave a different portion: one got five talents, the second got two talents, and the last got one talent. The first two workers went out and doubled their talents. The final worker buried the talent given to him. As the master returned, the first two workers turned in their increased portions. To them, the master stated, "Well done, good and faithful servants thou have been faithful over a few things, I will make thee ruler over many things; enter thou into the joy of the Lord" (Matthew 25:23).

When the last worker was presented, he told the master he was afraid and had hid the talent underground. The man was thinking solely of himself in his response: "And I was afraid and went and hid it in the earth, lo thou there have that is thine" (Matthew 25:25). His master was incredibly angry with his servant's manner of thinking. The master believed that the servant was selfish and unwise in handling the money which he was given. "Thou wicked and slothful servant, thou knewest that I reap where I sowed not. Thou ought to have put my money to the exchangers and then at my coming I should receive mine own with usury" (Matthew 25:26). There are two elements to this parable, in my humble opinion. The first is be not wary of small beginnings. The second: do not be afraid to use the talents which we are given, or they will be lost or given to someone else.

Your Destiny is Tied to Your Talent

My youth pastor and I enjoyed a close personal relationship. She would always be honest with me. I felt isolated from my core contacts when I relocated to the Midwest. The crossroads of life was beckoning. Emotionally, I felt like I was forgotten, and my situation was hopeless. My youth leader made two statements while doing a check in one day. She declared:

1. "You are currently in the backside of the desert."
2. "Your destiny is tied to your talent and it's not the talent you think."

What in the world! She appeared to be speaking in riddles. I lead my church's drama ministry. I often questioned that I could be doing more but rationalized there were many ways to get the message of Christ delivered. The medium of delivery I used was the stage. There were individuals at the time who stated, "You should be preaching by now." I had no interest in preaching in the traditional sense. The premise for the arguments of those who believed in my talents was rooted in the words of Jesus in the book of Luke 12:48, "...For unto whomsoever much is given, of him shall be much required: and to whom men have committed much of him they will ask the more." I won speech contests, staged dramas, co-edited the church's newsletter, and wrote poetry. Sometimes, I sought to be left alone. I wanted to exist in the shadows. What else should I be doing? The fact that there was a belief I should be doing more is sometimes construed that I was not performing fully in my intended gift.

My mom often says, "Nobody do yuh like yuh do yourself." This statement has proven true time and time again. As individuals, we are masters at creating obstacles for ourselves. We often doubt our talents, fear change, ignore instructions given by concerned friends, which at times, impede our development. There are periods when you think you have nothing to offer, or your gift is not enough. In these phases, you need to be dead to self-doubt and open to the leading of the Holy Spirit.

Glory to God

Our talent brings glory to God when it is utilized in the manner which it was intended. The parable of the barren fig tree explains this concept. The story is told in Luke 13:6-9. The fig tree remained fruitless for three years. The owner of the fig tree asked his gardener why the tree was without fruit. The gardener responded by requesting a year to till the soil so that it may bring forth fruit. However, he said if he were not successful and the tree bore no fruit it would be chopped down. Likewise, if we do not realize the value of our gifts, they too will be lost to us. God cannot be glorified in a fruitless state.

The talents and gifts which we are blessed with is an empowerment to complete our assignment. Like the fictional character Popeye, once he consumes a helping of spinach, he gains supernatural strength. Likewise, we become endued with fortitude when our talents are used as intended. Our tasks vary from one to another as no two missions are alike. The apostle Peter had this to say about using our gifts in service for God: “As every man hath received the gift, even so minister the same one to another, as good stewards of the manifold grace of God. If any man speak, let him speak as the oracles of God; if any man minister let if do it as of the ability which God giveth: that God in all thing may be glorified through Jesus Christ, to whom be praise and dominion for ever and ever. Amen” (1 Peter 4:10-11).

Your God-given gift is best realized before it gets buried in the graveyard.

Are you living up to your potential or to the expectations of others?

Does fear and doubt keep you hiding in the shadows?

Are you using your talents as they were intended by God?

*****

Food for Thought: Our purpose is to serve God with the talents we were blessed with. The eye cannot sing, and the ears cannot speak, each talent and ministry has a function within the body of Christ. Be not wary of small beginnings as all gifts matter to God, no talent is insignificant. The abilities we are blessed with allows us to represent God in all His glory.

God Isolates, So We Appreciate

"But they that wait upon the Lord shall renew their strength; they shall mount up with wings as eagles; they shall run, and not be weary; and they shall walk, and not faint."

Isaiah 40:31

Waiting. It is one of the hardest and most tedious tasks known to man in my opinion. If there is a detour on our normal route, we become uptight because we must wait for traffic to move along. Finding the shortest routes to our destination and trying to beat the red lights are just some of the ways in which we circumvent the aspect of waiting. We have become the microwave generation, and waiting is a virtue which has seemingly died a slow death. It has become such a fast-paced society that, if we should wait a minute for anything, we would consider it an inconvenience. Many of our friends in biblical times waited: Noah, Joseph, David, and Abraham. They all waited years on promises to be fulfilled by God.

A Watched Pot

God often uses different techniques in our waiting process, and some are disappointments, betrayals, hurt, or taking us from our comfort zones. It is God's way of directing us to where He wants us to go. My waiting periods have been made to feel like a pot that takes forever to boil. I have learned that your response to waiting often dictate the length of time for these phases in your life.

As a child, I loved spending the weekends with my aunt Jessica. She was an excellent cook and baker. I took pleasure in helping her prepare the batter for her cakes. Often, she would let me have the spoon and the bowl afterwards to "lick" it clean. I enjoyed eating from the bowl. However, the baking period took forever. I would always sneak in the kitchen to see the progress of the cake. It was hard waiting for a slice of her delicious cake. She would say, "A watched pot never cooks." I would become frustrated and impatient in my waiting period and storm out the kitchen. Similarly, when we are in holding patterns in our lives, it is made to feel like we are on a never-ending journey. In fact, waiting periods can be daunting but should never be viewed as wasted moments. The realization should be that waiting periods are a protection system from God as we can only enjoy small increments at once.

Some individuals hate to wait as there is a fear of the unknown and the sentiment that we have no control during this period. It is in these times that God isolates us from our comfort zones so we may trust him and learn to depend solely on him. There are periods in our waiting when we know what we need to do, but we are crippled by change and fear. In 2014 I was caught in such a waiting period.

Stones at the Bus Stop

I worked in a health care setting for adolescents and children that dealt with various concerns: suicide, physical abuse, and low self-esteem, among other issues. I led groups but often felt limited and that there was more that I could offer. I travelled by public transportation to work each day. My bus stop was in front of a public housing complex, and the neighborhood was known for car thefts and other crimes. One night in question, several boys began cat-calling me continuously while I stood at the bus stop. "Hey, Shorty," they shouted. I ignored their calls, and apparently, they were offended by my perceived rejection. Next thing I heard were stones hitting the pavement beside me. I realized that they were directly throwing stones at me, and I knew then that my days at this job was numbered.

The boys continued the throwing of stones in my direction. Several of them hit me on the back of the leg and arm. I prayed for the bus to arrive. This was my change moment; my waiting time was over, and I needed to leave this job. My answer came in the form of stones. I was dragging my feet, so God intervened. It was time to begin another chapter on my journey. Daniel was also in a waiting phase but in a different manner.

Daniel and the Angel

Daniel was in a foreign land in Babylon. He was taken from everything which was familiar to him. His only solace was communicating with God, and he had an appointed time each day. Daniel was fasting and praying for three weeks for the deliverance of the people from their immoral lives.

He received no response for his continuous prayers. Daniel held steadfast in his belief for an answer. His perseverance was rewarded as he finally got a visit from the angel who explained that his prayers were held up by the kingdom of Persia:

> Fear not Daniel: for from the first day that thou didst set thine heart to understand and to chasten thyself before God, thy words were heard, and I am come for thy words. But the prince of the kingdom of Persia withstood me one and twenty days; but, lo, Michael, one of the chief princes, came to help me; and I remained there with the kings of Persia.
>
> Daniel 10:12-13

Daniel was able to realize the reason for the delayed answer, and that God had in fact answered his prayer. Answers to our queries are sometimes delayed, but be patient as our waiting will not be in vain. While we wait, we should wait with a spirit of expectation and thanksgiving but not frustration.

*****

Food for Thought: God uses many things in our waiting period to get our attention. He is always is on time. We should wait with an attitude of joyful expectancy as laid out in Scripture. "For the vision is yet for an appointed time, but at the end it shall speak and not lie: thou it tarry, wait for it; because it will surely come, it will not tarry" (Habakkuk 2:3).

Cast the First Stone

"For I was hungered, and ye gave me meat; I was thirsty and ye gave me drink: I was a stranger, and ye took me in."
Matthew 25:35

In my junior year of undergrad, I walked into my advisor's office to inquire what I needed to do to change my major. Prior to walking into my advisor's office, I sat in a Sociology class entitled "Social Inequality." I was hooked. The problem, I was already on track to complete my degree in another department. My advisor looked at my course load and stated I would need another year and a half give or take to switch full time to Sociology. I thought about all the money that was invested in my current major with one year left to go and walked out the office, crestfallen. There died the dream of Sociology, but deep within the alcoves of my mind, there was always a call to help those in need.

A Shifting

I completed my degree and worked in an advertising agency in Manhattan. Traveling to and from work daily, I saw the need on the streets and in the train stations. The disparities did not escape me as I looked at the high-end shops along fifth avenue, but then, as I headed to the 34th train station, I saw the glaring poverty in the streets. The words of my mother echoed in my head, "One paycheck away from being homeless." I wanted to know what more I could do. The young man I dated at the time heard me say constantly, "I would love to find a graduate program that has a social conscience with a dramatic component." I became a broken record until I stopped speaking about it. Months later, I began receiving college applications in the mail from graduate programs. These were the days before the internet and Google. My friend requested the applications to be mailed to my address. I reviewed all the application booklets, and one area of study fit perfectly with my description: Drama Therapy.

I completed all the application requirements without doing any research on the program. I reasoned the name of the program was self-explanatory. One of the mandated requirements for graduating included going into individual therapy. All the other conditions were easily achieved, but the final requirement of going into individual therapy was not necessary, I recalled thinking. I remember telling my Program Director I did not need therapy; church is my safe place. He replied, "This is not a replacement for church, but if you are to help your clients you have to walk in their shoes." At that time in my thinking, going into therapy meant you had a mental illness, which carried a stigma. However, I realized it would be beneficial to my well-being and future, so I began individual therapy sessions.

The next hurdle was finding an internship site. I was accepted to be an intern in a Drop-in Center for Homeless Youth in Manhattan. The shelter dealt with clients who had a variety of issues, mental illness, questions about their sexuality, hunger, and abuse, among other issues. What had I gotten myself into? Homelessness, sexuality, and mental illness were all stigmas to be addressed. I recalled my days with Lillian and realized it would be a challenge, but one in which I overcame and learned lifelong lessons.

Gratitude, Humor, Respect, and Theft

Initially, I was not certain what to expect from the population at my internship site.

I was now on their home court, and I was scared and confused. That confusion stemmed from speculating how I would be received by my new clients. I was a minority like many of the program members, and I expected some resistance. However, I would soon become one of the "family." At the end of my internship, I felt as marginalized as they did. I experienced judgement by the public as I left the building daily. The shelter's presence was not welcomed in its location. I sensed it in the cold stares and stiff body language. There were many encounters which informed my learning, but there are two which have stayed with me to this day.

My first weeks were emotionally draining. I was tested, rejected, shunned, and I felt helpless. I rationalized these behaviors as their way of welcoming me into their world. I also viewed it as major resistance to me as a student intern. Two incidents happened within the first few weeks which made me realize that this was where I wanted to be, and this was the last place I should have been. An internal and external battle of wills existed within me.

The door to my workspace was accidentally left open by a colleague who had borrowed the space for a meeting. A program member entered the empty room unnoticed, went into my backpack, stole my purse, and used my credit card to go on a spending spree in Times Square. I saw this as a major test and an intrusion into my private space. I was torn between anger and compassion. However, I chose to be compassionate. The reality was they were homeless individuals who needed my help, and I was able to make a difference.

In my second encounter I was interning on Thanksgiving Day. The atmosphere inside the community room was pleasant, and the program members were calm. "This is a place for lost souls," one of the participants said. Upon closer inspection of this statement, I realized that everyone who came into the center was lost in one form or another. However, today everyone was on an equal playing field. We were all present to give thanks, play some games, watch a movie, and enjoy a meal together.

The following is a conversation which I had with a program member on Thanksgiving Day:

C*:* Happy Turkey Day, Mindy.
*MT***:** Thanks, C, same to you.
*C***:** Okay, check this out. How many turkeys went to the Thanksgiving Day party?
MT: Two turkeys went to the party.
*C***:** No, none because they are all on the dinner table (He clutches his stomach laughing)!
*MT***:** C, you are something else (I smile at him).
C**:** You know, I am glad to be here today because I was suspended from the building. That is no joke being outside in this weather. I did it for three days, and I am glad I am back.

I got very emotional after this conversation with C. I thought of the words of Christ, "In as much you have done it unto one of the least of these my brethren, you have done it unto me" (Matthew 25:40). I had somewhere to live, food to eat, and a loving family. He was thankful even though he did not know where his next meal after Thanksgiving was coming from. He reminded me to be grateful for the little things. Most importantly, I realized that I have never known what it is to experience hunger. We often use the phrases, "I am starving" or "I am so hungry," frivolously, but many individuals have never felt the pangs of real hunger knocking at their doors.

During my time at the internship site, I was able to show patience, tolerance, and be slow to anger. I realized I was being equipped with powerful life lessons as I walked in my clients' shoes. I was empathetic to their plight of being homeless and mentally ill. I might not agree with all their life's choices, but I realized it was not my place to judge, and they gained my respect. The homeless youth are just like everyone else. They are tenacious, intelligent, and resilient. They have emotions and ideas like certain members of the society which have viewed them as pariahs. Homelessness is not a disease; it is a predicament, and some members of the very society which shun them are just a paycheck away from this default if they are not financially careful. I often wondered the following:

> *Who will be the voice for the homeless youth?*
>
> *Is there a chance that you have been in contact with angels unknowingly within the homeless population?*
>
> *Who will be the voice for the unheard and the eyes of the unseen?*

Jesus and the Woman caught in Adultery *(John 8:1-11)*

The story is told of Jesus preparing to minister in the Temple, he sat down to teach the crowd. During his teachings, he was accosted by the Scribes and Pharisees the law makers of the day. They presented before him a woman who was caught in the act of adultery. These law makers questioned Jesus to trick him into answering as they had already broken the law by only arresting the woman. The Mosaic Law required both parties involved in the act to be stoned. Jesus ignored their question and quietly wrote in the dirt with his finger, ignoring them. He then said, "He that is without sin among you, let him cast the first stone." What powerful statement which proved to be introspective. One by one, her accusers exited the temple from the oldest to the youngest.

Jesus was left alone with the adulterous woman. He was aware of her sinful life, but He took mercy on her and offered forgiveness. She was told to go on her way and sin no more. He showed compassion in a situation which required punishment and ostracization, according to the laws of society. He also exposed the lawmakers as who they were, hypocrites of the times. As believers in Christ, we should strive not to walk in the footsteps of the Pharisees but display traits of love.

*****

Food for Thought: Walk a day in someone's shoes before you pass judgement. An act of kindness can have a positive impact on someone's life. We should strive to clean the garbage from our backyards before we attempt to judge others for their refuse. Remember God meets us where we are, as frail humans who need the gift of grace and mercy daily.

Run Your Race

"...And let us run the race with
patience that is set before us."

Hebrews 12:1

Sports Day

I am from a land known for a generation of great sprinters.

The tradition of running begins early in life in my country of birth. We are engaged in this practice from Basic school (Early Childhood) to the Tertiary level. We are always running. We had foot races on the streets to flex our competitive muscles. As youngsters, we ran to the store, ran to the river, ran to the bus stop—always running. At the time I attended my high school, it was known for its sprinting prowess. We produced runners who were recognized on a national and international level. I was not a sprinter, but I was familiar with the runners in my school. Our student athletes embodied hard work and determination to achieve the recognition they received.

The closest I ever came to being competitive in running was my high school sports day. My house leader needed someone to start the 4x100 relay and asked me to fulfill this duty. I figured he must have been desperate to ask me as I was not known for running. The team was to be anchored by a young lady, who at the time was at the top of her sprint class nationally. I was petrified. It is often said that it is not how you begin your race but how the race ends that is important.

In my estimation, if I did not run a good first leg, the pressure would be on the anchor person to work harder and we rise and fall as one. I did run my leg and performed credibly well; our relay team went on to win the race. My house leader would later say, after the race, that all he saw during my leg was my hair in the wind. In life, we are faced with many challenges along our path, and we should persevere until the end. These challenges prepare us to survive adversities but there is a trend which I have noticed which appears to nullify the aspect of working hard.

Winners All

I have noticed a troubling trend in today's society. Every young child that competes in an event receives a medal. From the first place to the last place person. I do not agree with this concept. Everything should be done within reason. The entire premise is that there should be healthy competition, and at the end of the race the best person wins. If on that day you were not at your best, then you go back to the drawing board and try again. I understand that children need encouragement, but they must not be lulled into a false sense of achievement. This practice can be perceived as deceptive. In essence, no effort is needed to gain the prize. The best of the best among elite athletes have failed and returned better because of their failure. As Christians, we should not adapt our race to the world's pace. Saul who was later known as the

Apostle Paul received a revelation as he attempted to continue his race of abuse of the believers in Christ.

Saul/Paul's Race

The Apostle Paul voiced: "Know ye not that they which run in a race run all but one recieveth the prize? So, run that ye may obtain. And every man that striveth for the mastery is temperate in all things now they do it to obtain a corruptible crown; but we an incorruptible" (1 Corinthians 9:24-25). The Life of the Apostle Paul has always fascinated me. He would have been a prime candidate to lecture in the halls of academia in today's world. He was highly intelligent, trained as a Pharisee which were the law makers of the day. Saul was known to be the persecutor of Christians. In fact, he witnessed and approved of the death of Stephen, who was the first known person to give his life for the Gospel of Jesus Christ. Saul, as he was then known, had made plans to commit further atrocities against believers of Jesus Christ. However, there was a roadblock to his plans. Along his race route, Saul was converted to Paul and the direction he envisioned his life taking changed forever.

Paul was blinded on the road to Damascus (Acts 9:1-7). He temporarily lost his physical sight but gained permanent spiritual vision. He went from persecutor of Christians to a staunch preacher of the Gospel of Jesus Christ. Similarly, we should be willing to alter goals in our race to achieve God's purpose. Our race in life is not always as we envisioned it to be. Situations, which society deem as the best, do not necessarily factor into God's race equation for our lives. Our race requires us to be wise, flexible, and patient. Each leg of the race we run entails a certain skill set and the awareness that it serves a purpose. The key is to focus on the leg which you were assigned to run.

Are you running the race which was laid out for you?

*****

Food for Thought: The realization that we each have a different race to run is paramount to our being and survival. We cannot all achieve a house, car, promotion, having a child, exotic vacations, or a marriage proposal at the same time. Each person has a different race schedule. Run the race you were meant to run.

Blessed

"She openeth her mouth with wisdom; and
in her tongue is the law of kindness."
Proverbs 31:26

Mothers are a blessing to those around them, whether biological or otherwise. My mother is one of the most practical, giving, loving, intelligent, and funny person I know. She never wavered in the face of pressure. Mom taught me about practicality, and it was on display every day. I remember my sister buying mom a fifteen-dollar singing card to celebrate an occasion. Singing cards were the new craze, and I was excited to see mom's face. Well I was in for a surprise. Mom opened the envelope and said, "Nice card, but you could have bought two cans of condense milk with the fifteen dollars." The air was let out the room. Years later, my sister would say she did not realize Mom's wisdom in the moment, but now that she had responsibilities of her own, she understood her practicality.

Pragmatic Lessons of Mom

My mom is known for doling out common sense wisdom. My brother and I knew what it meant to travel before we stepped on a plane. Mom would always be telling us "Go to

France" when we asked for an item which she deemed excessive. In other words, do not asks me for anything unnecessarily as I am providing for your needs. Or she would sneeze and asked if anything had fallen from her nostrils most times saying, "It drop yet?" However, my all-time favorite with mom was my asking for a new pair of school shoes even though the old ones were in good condition.

My only reason for wanting a new pair of shoes was that I had been wearing the Buster Browns for more than two years, and figured I should get a new pair. No matter what I did to damage the Buster Browns, they held firm. They were the strongest pair of shoes I ever had. She told me, "Of course you can get a new pair of shoes, go outside and choose a tree, any tree and pick all the leaves you can and take them to the store." That told me everything I needed to know. I was not getting the new shoes, and I should appreciate my old shoes. However, I did not always appreciate Mom's sacrifices.

Mom, a Cardboard Box, the Red Bag, and Market Day

Mom went to the market in Kingston every Saturday morning. Sometimes my brother went with her, but for the most part, Mom was on her own. She had her special vendors for meat, fruits, and produce. Mom had a red tarpaulin bag specifically made for market day instead of using a regular bag that was commonly used. I hated that bag. It was not stylish; in fact, it was ugly. She took the bag to most venues, and only church was the exception.

One Saturday, Mom took her red bag to the market and walked into a gun fight. She kept shopping away from the commotion until the shooting came closer to her. Then she dived into a cardboard box of bananas for protection as all the vendors and customers had left the area. The scene was pure chaos individuals were running everywhere. A man was seen by Mom, running towards the hospital with an injured person in his handcart. The street was littered with garbage and discarded produce. Mom peeped over the side of the box, the streets were deserted, and her knees and hands were bruised. She attempted to brush crushed bananas and packaging off her clothing.

Once she deemed the area safe, she picked up her bananas, which thankfully were not crushed and were already paid for. Then she collected her other produce and meats from her vendors and headed home. The incident was reported on the radio as headline news. However, when she got home, I briefly listened to her version of the incident and checked on her bruises. My prime interest was the contents of Mom's red bag. What was the bounty? Was it guineps, mangoes, naseberries, otaheite, apples, star apples, or plums? Mom always had a plan. She risked her safety and displayed a will to survive. She made a sacrifice, so her family would be provided for. Likewise, Jochebed was a mother with a master plan.

Jochebed the Mother with a Plan

In the land of Egypt, the children of Israel were great in number and were perceived to be powerful. There was a new Pharaoh in Egypt, and he felt threatened by the growing population of the Israelites. So, he decided to plant words of discord. He told his people that the children of Israel would revolt against them someday. This would be the part of the earliest rumor mill formed. The Pharaoh then established a plan to control the population. He asked the midwives to throw all male babies into the Nile. "And Pharaoh charged all his people, saying, Every son that is born ye shall cast into the river, and every daughter ye shall save alive" (Exodus 1:22). He was sure his plan would be successful.

Moses' mom, Jochebed, planned with her daughter Miriam to hide the baby Moses in a basket and placed him among the reeds in the river. One day Pharaoh's daughter came to take a bath and heard the crying child. She took pity on him. Miriam, his sister stepped forward and offered the assistance of her mom without Pharaoh's daughter being any wiser of her identity. "Then said his sister to Pharaoh's daughter, Shall I go and call to thee a nurse of the Hebrew women, that she may nurse the child for thee?" (Exodus 2:7).

Miriam brought Jochebed to Pharaoh's daughter. She was asked to assist in Moses' upbringing. Jochebed was being paid by the enemy to perform a job she would have freely done. Her plan saved the life of her child. When he was of age, she brought Moses to Pharaoh's daughter's house to reside. His mother made the ultimate sacrifice. The irony of her plan, having the enemy raise her child, who later in his life liberated the nation of Israel from the very household that raised him and prosecuted his people.

*****

Food for Thought: Mothers are ingenious, intelligent, kind, and funny. They should be loved and appreciated. They are willing to make sacrifices for their children, which at times can be detrimental to their health and safety. Mothers are a blessing—hats off to them.

Withstand Your Shaking

"The Lord will give strength unto his people;
the Lord will bless his people with peace."
Psalm 29:11

Fear is the evil twin of faith. It also has a few friends in the form of doubt, worry, and low self-esteem. If we look at fear in today's terms, it would be the big bad bully in the school yard. Fear paralyzes and keeps us from trusting God. There were many action songs that I would sing on Sunday in reference to shaking or dancing in a manner of praise. There was no fear, just childlike exuberance. However, my family members and I would experience a shaking which re-enforced the power of God and how we react as individuals in times of uncertainty.

The Land of Machu Pichu

My sister, myself, and our nephew decided we would visit Peru. We had an awesome experience even though I experienced altitude sickness. Peru has amazing food, fruits, seafood, beautiful culture, accommodating people, and churches galore. God was on display in all His glory with the majestic mountains and a variety of many agricultural produces. The many different arrays of corns and potatoes were amazing. It also had beautiful flowers and amazing wildlife.

We had plans to visit Lima and Cusco. While in Lima, we did experience an actual shaking. A magnitude 8.0 earthquake struck the country. We were not close to the epicenter, but we were able to feel the shaking. Our nephew, my sister, and I were asleep at the time of the quaking. My sister and I woke up during the shaking. However, our nephew slept through the entire incident. While awake, we were both calm, and I exclaimed, "Oh well, God got us." My sister agreed, and we stayed awake briefly to see if they needed us to evacuate our room. We heard no one knocking for evacuation, so we returned to sleeping. Our nephew awoke in the morning, oblivious to what had occurred overnight.

During breakfast, the guests at the hotel made the earthquake the main topic of discussion. Fear and anxiety were evident on some of the faces of the guests. A few were heard discussing checking out of the hotel. Others were busy planning their excursions for the day. The responses of everyone to the earthquake made me think of how we respond to shakings or disturbances in our daily lives. We could react in one of the following ways:

- *We could become anxious and fearful because of the perceived uncertainty.*
- *We could be oblivious and endure the shaking.*
- *We could be aware of the shaking, knowing that God is in control.*

My sister and I chose the latter response, and it have served me well in my life challenges.

Sickness

In recent times, I have faced multiple shakings. However, God's presence has been felt every step of the way. I was diagnosed with strep throat which manifested with a fever and spots, and I needed to be medicated. After my strep throat diagnosis, I was laid off from my job. As I dealt with the loss of my job, I learned that one of my former coworkers lost a family member. After visiting doctors for my yearly appointments, I was told that further tests would be needed. During the testing I was informed a former co-worker had died. The hits kept coming.

I completed the bloodwork, and various tests needed all gave favorable results. However, my doctor and I decided on minor surgery to be certain of a diagnosis. My doctor tried to calm me by saying it was "minor" surgery. My reply was, "There is no such thing as minor surgery." I became mentally tired and wanted 2019 to end. However, I remembered a friend would always say, "If He brings you to it, He will take you through it." So, with renewed trust, I live day to day in God's hands.

The Pandemic

These health challenges, deaths, and loss of my job paled in comparison to what was in store as the Coronavirus paid us a visit. That was a shaking unto itself. A shaking from complacency and compromise, if you will. It enabled me to appreciate solace, family, and simplicity. During this trying time of the virus, it felt as if it was a warning to break up our folly ground as a people. Conversely, although the Coronavirus presented many challenges, such as, but not limited to, loss of income, economic shutdown, and death, it also served as a time for revelations, appreciation, and reflections. In this period, I have learned the following:

- *As individuals, we do not need half the resources we think we do.*
- *God is our only source for daily survival.*
- *This time of reflection may be viewed as a time to stop and appreciate the simple things.*
- *Now is not the time to take our eyes off God.*

Guess what? God does not sleep.

God knew we would be in a pandemic years before it became a reality. I have utilized the time to reflect on my relationship with others and God. Life has changed as we know it forever, but if we are not willing to alter behaviors then our shaking would have been in vain. I have allowed myself to question many of these Earth Runnings in my finite mind and often wonder, *Why me?* However, amid all this shaking, the one constant belief I have had is that *God is in control*! There is a lesson in all the shaking experiences, and we will be better for wear if we trust and believe in God. The shaking can be viewed as preparation for better things ahead as proven by Job; he endured and overcame his shaking.

Job, His Friends, and Wife

One of the greatest examples of being shaken in the Bible can be viewed in the life of Job. He was a man of faith, and he enjoyed a wealthy lifestyle. In today's world, Job would have been on the "Ten Richest People in the World" list. However, Job experienced a shaking of epic proportions without any

Glossary

The Proverbs and sayings are written in Patois (pronounced Pat-wah), the dialect spoken in the island of Jamaica.

Chapter: The Good Samaritan

Jamaican Proverb**:** "Scarnful dawg nyam dutty pudding"
Translation**:** Scornful dog eat dirty pudding

A "mad person"—Mentally ill street person or homeless person

Chapter: Gratitude is Essential

Jamaican Proverb: "Cow neva know di use a him tail til him lose it"
Translation: Cow never know the use of his tail until he loses it

Fart—"Passing Gas"/Flatulence

Bully Beef—Canned Corn Beef

"Dad talk di truth a yuh fart—Dad be truthful you "passed gas"

Chapter: Blink of an Eye

Di—The

Yuh—You

Awright yuh cool—All right you cool

Chapter: You are More Than

"Rapping"—A T.V. Program for young people

Brain Fart—A temporary mental lapse

Earth Runnings—Daily Happenings

Chapter: Word Power

Jamaican Proverb: "Kibba yuh mouth man"
Translation: Close your mouth

Chapter: Case of Mistaken Identity

Jamaican Proverb: "Yuh shake man hand, yuh nuh shake him heart"
Translation: You shake man hand; you do not shake his heart

Chapter: Potentially Talented

Duppy—Ghost

Chapter: Unwelcomed Spirits

Obeah—Black Magic/Black Arts

Balm yard—A place where healing rituals of obeah are practiced

Chapter: Suffer the Little Children

Small up yuhself—Make room or space for someone else

Gypsy—Secret Code (like Pig Latin)

Dutty Pot—Making mud Pies (Child's play form of cooking)

Run a Boat—Cooking a Meal with Friends (with whatever ingredients you can find)

Robots—Illegally run buses

Schoolers—School Children

Chatter Box—Someone that talks excessively

Wash—A drink similar to lemonade (made with water and brown sugar)

Chapter: Stranger in a Strange land

Browning—a term used to define a lighter complected individual most commonly used on females

Baby love—a term which would typically be heckled as a greeting from a street corner (like catcalling)

Chapter: For your Good

Wash Out—Herbal cleansing

Yuh—You

Fi—For

Bibliography

Author Unknown, "Speak the Truth," research seemingly attributed the Poem to Henry William Dulcken. 1832-1894.

Mindy Tucker, "Sands of Time," in *Love by Nature*, Ed(s) Joan Celestine, Sandra Wright, Meran Senior, Netheline Bennett, (South Carolina: Amazon Createspace, 2014) pp. 28.

Mindy Tucker, "Shades of Grey," in *Love by Nature*, Ed(s) Joan Celestine, Sandra Wright, Meran Senior, Netheline Bennett, (South Carolina: Amazon Createspace, 2014) pp. 198-199.

About the Author

Earth Runnings, Revelations and Grace is the author's first book. She has a Master of Arts in Drama Therapy from New York University. The author has worked with various populations in the Healthcare and Early Childhood setting. She loves traveling, writing poetry, and has served as the leader for her church drama ministry. Several of her poems are included in a published collection entitled "Love by Nature."

CPSIA information can be obtained
at www.ICGtesting.com
Printed in the USA
LVHW020219130421
684331LV00005B/119